STUCK IN THE

A Generation X View of Talent Management

Curtis L. Odom, Ed.D.

I0074538

Book • nol • o • gy

A BUSINESS & EDUCATIONAL IMPRINT FROM ADDUCENT
www.Adducent.co

Titles Distributed In
North America
United Kingdom
Western Europe
South America
Australia

Stuck in the Middle

A Generation X View of Talent Management

Curtis L. Odom, Ed.D.

Hardcover ISBN: 978-1-937592-05-9
Paperback ISBN: 978-1-937592-15-8

Published by Booknology (a business and educational imprint from Adducent)

Jacksonville, Florida

www.Adducent.co *(that's right, it's not a .com)*

Published in the United States of America

TABLE OF CONTENTS

DEDICATION

To my wife and best friend Nelia – Your boundless support and undying belief in me through this incredible journey enabled a thought to grow into an idea, and an idea into the career changing reality that is my first book. I share my success in achieving this life milestone equally with you. I cannot imagine this world without you or my life without your love.

To my daughter Alyssa –I knew from the moment I held you in my arms that I would move mountains to keep you safe, walk miles just to see your smile, and wake up every morning eager to go to work at the most important job I will every have of being your Dad. Every day you remind me of the true joys of life and how with each experience, whether the outcome is good or bad, we learn something new.

ACKNOWLEDGMENTS

I would like to express my deepest appreciation for the unwavering support of my publisher, and friend, Dennis who created an environment in which I was able to explore without boundaries both the idea and practice of becoming a published author. His steady hand, sense of humor, and perspective on life as a Navy veteran were a match for my style from day one. Thank you, Dennis for your partnership, mentoring, and coaching through one of the most challenging years of my career. You inspired me to live and write with the Navy core values of Honor, Courage, and Commitment.

To my mother, Hilda, thank you for all of your love and support. I am grateful for your wisdom and guidance through my formative years. Your love is truly are a blessing in my life as I always felt your hand on my shoulder through the darkest nights of life as both a boy and a young man. Thanks Mom for everything.

Thanks to my brother-in-law, Hillard for instilling in me the value of education and the importance of not being satisfied with anything less than my best. As the male role model in my personal life, I continue to aspire to follow the example you have set. Your work ethic, creativity, and keen eye for all that is possible dared me to achieve. Your prophetic words to me long ago sound in my ear as my mantra when the toughest of life and career obstacles present themselves ... *"Short term inconvenience for long-term gain."* Brown Dawg, you are my hero!

To my sister, Betty; my mother-in-law, Lucia; my father-in-law, Afonso; and my sister-in-law, Allison; – Thank each of you for all of your love, encouragement, patience and support. You guys are the greatest cheerleading squad one could ever hope to have on the sidelines. Your faith and confidence in my success will remain legendary.

To Strive, To Seek, To Find, and Not To Yield - Tennyson

INTRODUCTION

I think the best way to teach is to provide examples ... preferably real and not hypothetical ones constructed purely for the sake of telling a story. Real experiences. Real events. Real Decisions ... with real outcomes. *"What happened, what I did, and what happened next" kind of examples.* That is how I've approached this book you have in your hands. There will be some, what I feel are astute, observations, as a Gen Xer, on life and certainly on career but these are only part of what I will share with you.

From the age of four to twelve a lot happened in my life that made me who I am today. It was a foundation my teen years added to, until age eighteen when I joined the Navy, where I served for ten years. Those young adult years I spent exploring the world and learning about myself while in the military helped form me as a man. And the subsequent years after my time in uniform up to my current age, added layers of complexity to my life such as completing my formal education, and gaining critical career experience that have helped me answer a few crucial questions. Questions of *"Can I be my authentic self at work?" "What do I want in my career?" "How do I not get stuck in the middle?"* and, *"If I do get stuck ... how do I get unstuck?"*

It's the questions above that point succinctly to what many Gen Xers seek for themselves or seek as an answer from others. Perhaps this book will help you too, if you are seeking those same answers.

* * *

STUCK IN THE MIDDLE

I meet a lot of people who, like me, are Gen Xers. Most are stuck in the middle. They're gridlocked in the career traffic jam behind slow moving Baby Boomers who are tapping their breaks nonstop with impatient Millennials in their rearview mirror tailgating and making obscene finger gestures. And as they stew, they're trying to figure out, *How do I make it in corporate America?* I've had some success in very large companies and have reached fairly high-level positions for being only in my thirties. So some people seek me out and ask questions such as:

"What does it take to get to where you are?"

"How did you do it?"

"Did you have to sell your soul, or strike a deal with the devil?"

"What did you trade away in an effort for quick success?"

And I answered their questions by telling them the simple truth... my career story. I tell them that my success is directly tied to the decisions I've made in my career. I am speaking specifically of a series of choices of what to do and more importantly, what not to do. They look at me quizzically and say, "*Well, can you be more specific?*"

And in answering that final question, I always end up telling a little bit about my life story. I don't give a complete autobiography. I don't share every single event that went on in my life. But I do share with them some major facets; the scaffolding, if you will, that has given me a means to climb (and work from) since I was four—when I first had a real consciousness of authentic self that was established by pivotal and instrumental events in my life—until today.

I tell them part of my story, because I think it helps ground them with the fact I am just like them ... or like anybody else for that matter. I have made mistakes and have made choices that led to success. I have done a lot of dumb things that nobody saw but me and I've done some pretty dumb things that were on full display to the world. I've done a lot of things where I've said, *"I wish I didn't do that."* I've done a lot of things where I've said, *"I should have done that sooner."* But I do not have any instances in my life where I say *"Why didn't I do that?"* or *"I wonder what that opportunity could have turned into?"* Hopefully you see this as me being just like anybody else but I will point to one thing that makes me different than many.

I don't have work-related regrets or run from taking calculated career risks.

What I do that others don't is to study what went well for those I know and respect and try to replicate it. And I study what didn't go well so I can avoid it. That's it. I know that sounds simple and obvious but in my experience most Gen Xers don't do that. They don't scrutinize or self-assess themselves as honestly as they should. And I do. I feel you should be the most honest with yourself—if you can't get that right, then even with the right answers provided to you from mentors and coaches—then even with the best advice in the world you will not be successful.

I also seek feedback relentlessly. I believe everybody has it wrong with that old adage practice makes perfect; I don't think that's true. I think practice without feedback makes at best a mediocre performance permanent. Worse yet, if at practice you are missing the mark but have no guidance on how to correct yourself—then you run a high-probability risk of being off target when your best performance is required.

There's a distinction I've heard from the accomplished smart folks I follow in terms of my reading and my own professional development. Practice without feedback makes permanent, but only practice with feedback will make perfect. That's what I try to do. I have put that under my hat and carried with me everywhere I have gone. It has paid dividends for me. Now let me say some of that feedback was delivered with painful, mean-spirited, and sometimes, downright bigoted undertones. But I took each punch to the chin as a way to get to the truth of who I was perceived to be so that I could make positive changes in how I came across to others. What I found, however, is that my Baby Boomer (and some Gen Xer) colleagues were confirming for me over and over again the very suspicion I had all along. They confirmed that I was laboring to be some place that I did not really want to be. Chasing after what I did not really want and working hard at being someone that I really was not and would never be comfortably. I was working hard at not being my authentic self.

Some of what I'm going to share with you in the scope of this book, centers on what does talent management mean to a member of Generation X in the current workforce. What does it mean to be somewhere in your mid-to-late thirties or early forties and wondering is this all your career is supposed to be. Where is the meat in the sandwich? Or as the late Clara Peller (in the Wendy's commercials many years ago) used to famously ask, "where's the beef?'

I've worked hard to get to a specific place of success, by many standards, in my career, only to reflect on what it was really like once I got there. Some Gen Xers like me, got to that place, looked around and said, *"Okay, this is great and all, but I sacrificed a lot to get to this place—was it really worth it? What did I do, lose, or ignore to get me to this place of supposed happiness?"* What does it mean when you've spent the last ten years working really hard for your success and then on the day of your great achievement, you're so overwhelmed at the accomplishment you become disillusioned by it? And then six months after achieving that epic career milestone that you alone set, you find yourself disenfranchised while looking back and wondering. *"At what expense did I come by this strange new fortune?"*

All of these deep personal questions I have asked myself and my answers will be on full display and will hopefully resonate with you in your reading of this book. I know I am not unique in having these questions. So when other people ask me, *"How did you get there? What did you do? What choices did you make?"* The simple answer is that I am a product of everything that I have experienced to date in my life. And that is a perfect segue to talk to you a little bit about a couple of periods in my life in the next chapter.

CHAPTER ONE

Early Challenges & Self-Discovery

It's your life, your one and only life – so take excellence very personally.

– Scott Johnson

I was born in the capital city of the smallest state in the union, Providence, Rhode Island. My mother was thirty-six years old when I was born. My father was an active member of the family. I was fortunate not to be from a broken home and was lucky to not have the specter of divorce hanging over me as a child like so many of my Gen Xer friends, peers, and colleagues had when they were very young. I had two loving parents but that doesn't mean my childhood wouldn't be without its share of challenges and disappointments.

I started my career journey, as many of us do, with pre-school. Or at that time, I guess it might have been called nursery school. That's where I first learned hard work, studying and academic achievement was something expected in my family. I'll explain more about this shortly.

My Mom and father (whom I affectionately called Pop) both worked hard at their jobs. Pop was a spot welder and he worked from 6:00am until 2:30pm. My Mom worked the opposite shift—she was a receptionist at a hospital and would work from four in the afternoon until midnight. Sometimes, depending on shift needs, she'd work the 3:00pm to 11:00pm shift. But mostly my Mom's schedule when I was growing up was spent with her working the four to midnight shift.

Like most kids who were Gen Xers, my Mom would get me ready in the morning and take me to school. She'd drop me off then go home and do housework, run errands, grocery shop ... all those things that need doing to run a household—regardless of who did them. She would pick me up at 2:45pm and bring me home. I'd be home from about 3:00pm with my Mom, until she would leave around 3:30pm to head to work. Well, my Pop would get out of work at 2:30pm and probably get home right around three as he worked farther away from our house. I would have about twenty-five minutes with both my Mom and my Pop each day before they parted company—my Mom to go to work, and my Pop to make dinner and take care of me, especially seeing I got to bed when I needed to. I remember this ebb and flow of my young life distinctly. That's what it was like during the week. I'd see Mom during the morning, I'd see her when I got home, and I'd be home with my Pop in the evening. This was the routine schedule with my parents that shaped my young life.

My Pop was a man's man and a stern one at that. This guy just did not play around. He made sure I took education seriously. That was important to him because he did not have the opportunity to get more than a sixth-grade education. He was determined I would get more schooling than that and achieve more in life than he. In the short time my father was in my life, he was adamant that I take school seriously.

At nursery school if a kid was acting out, or was the class clown (a craft I perfected early in my career) they got put in "time out"—which, back then, they didn't really call it that. They would put you in an area of the playground and made you stay there. There was this structure on the playground at nursery school, and it was made out of some concrete tubes of different sizes they had put together and painted and put a little red brick chimney on to make it look like a train. When you got in trouble at nursery school during recess, you had to go sit on the caboose of the train until you calmed down or the teacher felt you had been sufficiently banished enough to come back to the large group. My Pop never took kindly to hearing from my Mom that I was told to go sit on the train or if I didn't do well. My Pop would paddle my hide but good to make sure I knew that was unacceptable behavior. Back then, corporal punishment of a child by their parent wasn't looked on as being abusive; it was part of what parents did in the raising of their children. So I got the belt plenty of times when Pop deemed I was not giving my all at school and not paying attention. Did I mention that this was nursery school?

Many times when I got a spanking, I know I deserved it. I had it coming. But it was always across the butt never anything across the face or some other part of the body. Back then; having a sore backside was more of an indication of love from your parents than abuse of you by them. My Mom came to realize she couldn't tell my father every time that, *"Curtis was on the train today,"* or *"He didn't listen in school today,"* or *"The teacher wanted to talk to me after school about Curtis throwing rocks at recess."* Yeah, that never went well. I think she was worried for my safety once when it seemed that I was getting a spanking every day one week. I don't know what it was, but apparently the message didn't get through to me that week. My Pop was a strict man when it came to my behavior in school because he loved me. He wanted me to be more than he ever was and that meant toeing the line in school and with him. So that was the school week—daily handoffs so that each day I could spend time with both my Mom and Pop. They made it work, and I loved them for making time for me.

Pop never drank, but he did smoke a pack—unfiltered—of Pall Mall cigarettes a day. That would be a contributing factor in determining the short period of time I had with my Pop in my life. He was from Mobile, Alabama and grew up in an area of the country and in a time where cooking a meal meant deep-frying. Plenty of the meals he prepared and ate were fried. Fried chicken, fried eggs, fried bacon, fried pork chops. To think of it, just about everything my Pop made and ate was fried. We are talking about old school country cooking that was real bad for you. We've all come to realize now, that deep fried food should be an infrequent treat... a brief taste of nostalgia, but not part of our recommended daily nutrition. We have all seen trans-fat become taboo—we have even seek Kentucky Fried Chicken become "KFC" because the very word "fried" has become the new "f-bomb".

As a result of my Pop eating a lot of fried foods (I recall chicken being fried in Crisco) and high-cholesterol foods—compounded with heavy smoking, my Pop wasn't in the best of health internally. He was a giant of a man; 6'4", a big guy, working in hot conditions all day, breathing in I don't know what in terms of fumes or smoke or gases. His work, his diet and his pack a day smoking all contributed to his poor respiratory and cardiac health.

My Pop also used to gamble; but maybe I shouldn't say gamble, because it seemed he always won. On Fridays he would get out of work early—I think it's because he worked so many hours during the week he was able to knock off a little bit early. He'd get out around noon. There is a street in Providence called Diamond Street, which still exists today, but back in the '70s the neighborhood around Diamond Street was where most blacks from South Providence would go. There'd be gambling in the form of poker games, and dice games. It was this whole street and I guess it was like an illegal block party. Every Friday, they had four or five different houses where people would sell beer, quarts of bootleg southern moonshine, and those "funny" cigarettes. Today, that kind of stuff would be broken up quickly, but back then, it was a social thing. There were never any stabbings, shootings, or drama that made the 11:00pm news, so the cops left it and them alone.

It was an area where blacks in the area who were probably about ten years removed from the fighting in the south during the civil rights movement could get together and let their collective afros down and relax around people who looked like them. Every Friday for two or three hours, my Pop would be at the dice table *"just taking those poor chaps money"* on Diamond Street. But my Pop would still come home at the time he was expected to every Friday. He'd do the child care change of command and take care of me so Mom could go off to work.

What I remember most about those Fridays is that every week my Pop would come home, walk into the kitchen, and throw a huge pile of money on the table. I didn't really realize what money was at that time, but I knew a lot of anything when I saw it. Some of that money I am sure was his weekly paycheck, but there was a lot more there than I would to this day imagine my Pop would have been paid as a spot welder in the '70s. I remember my Mom often saying, *"There's over a thousand dollars here."* That was a lot of money, especially in the '70s. I don't know how my Pop did it, but he was a winner. Every Friday he would cash his paycheck, head over to Diamond Street, and turn it into a lot more than that in a couple of hours. Of course, it wasn't something that was talked about, or that I could confirm, but I would gather that my Pop had a bit of a reputation of being a shark. I do know he was politely (because of his size) known for knowing how to win, or for only playing the games at which he knew he wouldn't lose.

That was how I remember and have come to understand who my father was as a provider financially for his family first above all things. The means might have been questionable, but the intent was honorable.

My Pop came home sick one afternoon in February of 1977. That odd day would later become one terrible night for all of us. My Pop wasn't well and my Mom, from working in a hospital all those years and seeing so much sickness, knew he didn't seem right when he came home from work that day. He looked ashen and wanted to rest. He even complained of being dizzy. That was a tip off to my Mom, if my Pop ever even said he was sick, there was something really wrong. My Pop was never sick. Being sick was a sign of weakness to and as such, it was something he never displayed. That afternoon, for that very reason, my Mom said, *"Listen, I'm not going to go to work today."* Pop said, *"Go ahead on to work. I ain't sick they just worked me too hard today."* My Mom said, *"No, you don't look right. I feel like I better be here."* So she called in that day, and it was a good thing she did. After dinner that evening my father collapsed in the bathroom upstairs. I remember a flurry of phone calls and frantic activity as my Mom tried to get him to sit upright. I remember her yelling at me with tears in her eyes to get dressed as my godmother (the wife of my Pop's best friend) along with all of our neighbors soon showed up at our house. I watched my Pop being carried out of the bathroom on a stretcher, down the stairs, out of our house, into an ambulance and rushed to the hospital with me in my godmother's Buick racing behind it. My Mom went in the ambulance with my Pop. It was all a tear-filled blur.

11

STUCK IN THE MIDDLE

Every time I see flashing lights and hear a siren, I think of that night in 1977.

We were at the hospital for what felt like a day but probably wasn't even four hours. I must have fallen asleep in the ER waiting room. Then sometime after midnight, after we'd been waiting for what seemed an eternity; my Mom woke me. She said, *"Curtis, Pop left us."* That was hard for me to hear back then. It is hard for me to say to this day, *"Pop left us."*

No way. I knew my Pop. My Pop wouldn't go anywhere without me or without my Mom, because he never had and just never would. So the follow up words of *"Pop went home to heaven"* haunt me to this day, over 30 years later. I was four-years old when my father passed away on February 27th of 1977. The following first week of March his son of the same name turned five years old. My Pop died of a massive coronary. He died from the lethal combination of noxious fumes, unfiltered cigarettes, and a diet of fried foods. My Pop was to be 49 years old that coming October.

I think of my Pop often. I am one of those nostalgic Gen Xers who like to watch old TV shows from the '70s and '80s. It's funny, I get home now late from work some nights and I'll flip on TVLand™ and catch an old episode of *Sanford and Son*, and I think fondly of my Pop. When he "looked after me" at night, after dinner, after he got me washed up, we would watch TV together until it was time for me to go to bed. Sometimes he'd let me stay up a little bit later. Most of the times when he let me stay up it was to watch *Sanford and Son*. We would watch it and just laugh. Mostly it was me laughing at him laughing, because of course I didn't understand the subtleties of the bigotry that the curmudgeon Fred G. Sanford, portrayed by Redd Foxx, often interjected into this sitcom. I loved that time with my Pop—just laughing with him, watching *Sanford and Son*. When I watch *Sanford and Son* now and any of the other primetime shows from back then, wherever I am, for those few moments, my Pop is with me ... sitting next to me laughing out loud.

My father's death set in motion a lot of things in my life. I'm sure you can tell by now how much I looked up to him. He was a strong, demanding man, as I mentioned, and he was my hero. This guy could do it all. He could laugh, joke, and curse with his friends. I will never forget the way we'd laugh at the *Three Stooges* as we hung out together early on Sunday mornings. After we got a good dose of slapstick comedy, we would go out and get the Sunday paper. Pop would take me with him for a ride in his green, Oldsmobile Delta 88 with the white leather seats through Roger Williams Park in Providence. When we got back, Mom would have breakfast ready for us. We'd sit there and eat like two old chums rather than father and son. We shared this insatiable appetite for homemade country biscuits and syrup with bacon. To this day, nothing says Sunday morning to me like country biscuits and syrup with bacon.

I sometimes wonder if he knew his time with me was short. The way he treated me like his little buddy those weekend mornings as opposed to a son was impactful and shaped the way I live my life, and raise my own daughter as a direct result. I live and laugh each day with her like it will be my last. Being with her, spending quality time together makes each day for me worth living. Seeing everything through her eyes gives me a daily renewal of hope and optimism for the world. It allows me to now be a Pop, to be who I have missed deeply, who I work hard every day to make proud of me in his absence.

From age five to eight, was really like looking out of the window of the Acela between New Haven and Providence ... a blur. There was a period of time, my Mom later told me, I was inconsolable, and she did not know what to do—she was dealing with her own grief and me with mine, as well. How was she going to take care of her son each night when she had to be at work? How would she raise a son without him having a father figure?

That was a time that became another important formative event in my young life, one that came on the heels of and as a result of my father's death. Seeing my Mom work hard—trying to keep her job and keep our household together, as well as getting me ready to go into first grade at a private school. My aunts and uncles all helped with me and an aunt moved in with us from when I was five-and-a-half until I was ten years old. This allowed my Mom to continue working four to midnight and sent me to private school. I never knew how my Mom was able to send me to private school, pay for a house, pay for uniforms—pay for all these things on a receptionist's salary. But I later figured it out.

It was because of all that money my Pop would bring home and pile up in the middle of our kitchen table. My Mom was smart enough to have saved all of that money. She would stash the money in the house over the weekend, and on Monday morning go up to the corner bank—at that time it was the Old Stone Bank—and put most of the money into the family account. I will never forget that, because the Flintstone characters were the registered trademarks of that bank like the Peanuts characters are today for MetLife. And of course, after my father passed away, we would receive his Social Security check every month. That money coming in, coupled with what was in the bank courtesy of Diamond Street, and her own salary helped my

Mom with the bills and the mortgage and covered sending me to private school. Though it was hard on her, my Mom made it work. While I don't remember a whole lot about my childhood from age five to eight, I will certainly never forget one family bus trip.

When I was five years old, my Mom, aunt and I went to Louisiana to where my Mom is originally from to see my grandmother and grandfather. That visit became the genesis of the conversation with one of my aunts that later led to her coming to Rhode Island to live with us. We flew down to New Orleans on Eastern Airlines and I got a chance to meet my grandfather, my Mom's father. He was a great guy. He smoked a pipe and he taught me how to whittle. I'd never heard of whittling before, but he taught me how to whittle. He would sit there and I remember him asking, *"So, tell me about where you're from. Tell me about what it looks like. Tell me about what you see when you look out your front door. Tell me what you see when you look out your bedroom window. What's your favorite food to eat there?"* He would ask me all of these great questions that were all about me. He never told me a whole bunch about himself, but he asked me all about me and I liked that. I thought that was great, because no one else asked about me. Not like that. So I spent a week with him and then we flew home. Then when my Mom would call down to her home to talk to her parents, there was always time allowed for me to talk to "Paw-Paw" to see how he was doing. He'd ask me, *"So everything is going all right?"* We had a five-minute conversation and I looked forward to that, because somebody so far away in a place I had never been wanted to talk to me. That special long-distance relationship would continue for three years until tragedy again would rob me of a second father figure.

My grandfather passed away when I was eight years old. My Mom, my aunt (who was living with us by this time) and I returned to Louisiana. Back then I remember it being really expensive to fly—so we didn't get to fly that time—and we didn't take a train. We instead took a Greyhound bus from Providence, Rhode Island, to [Kentwood], Louisiana. It took three-and-a-half days and was probably one of the worst experiences of my young life. On a bus as an 8-year old for that long—from Podunk to Podunk town—all the way down to Louisiana. Having to go to the bathroom in that moving, steel death trap on the bus they call a bathroom. Sitting in different bus stations waiting for the connecting bus (that was always late) and feeding quarters into those old black and white televisions attached to stationary chairs in the bus stations. The novelty of this made the circumstance almost bearable ... getting to watch TV in bus stations in towns I didn't even know existed was surreal. I remember that experience because it taught me how to put up with just about anything—and everything. It taught me patience. It taught me to always keep a couple of quarters in your pocket.

It taught me that you're not always in control and to just deal with it.

We made it to Louisiana and were there for a week. The family homestead there had fallen into great disrepair due to "Paw-Paw" having been ill before his death. It was nothing like what I remembered from my first visit just three years earlier.

This time, I met all of my cousins, on my Mom's side of the family. They had descended like locusts on the house due to the death in the family. All the folks I'd heard of while listening to (eavesdropping on) conversations between my Mom and my aunt but never really knew. And to this day these are people whom I believe I would have done just fine without ever knowing or having met in person. I know that must sound horrible, but allow me to qualify that statement in the next few paragraphs.

What was harsh about this experience, was that it was painfully obvious and evident to me, and to them that I was different. To them, I was this spoiled, rich kid from the North who talked fast and proper, that had all of these matching clothes, new shoes (growing up as an only child I never wore a hand-me-down)—many things they did not have. There I was in a place where people had to wait in line to take a bath in the evening. And you had to boil water for your hot bath. And where every time someone boiled bath water, there were at least two to three bathers slated for that bath. It wasn't where you could take a shower—there wasn't any hot running water or heat in the house. There were about twenty people now staying in Paw-Paw's six-room house that had an indoor bathroom annexed by a genuine wooden outhouse.

It was a jarring change for me to go from my house in New England, where I had my own room, plenty of hot water, and a working toilet – to basically a third world country. And all of this was coupled with meeting people, my extended family, who treated me like anything but. That week was one of the worst weeks of my young life. Compounding the sadness of losing my Paw-Paw, I had to endure my cousins, aunts, and uncles constantly making fun of me because of the way I talked. My cousins stole most of my clothes. I was pushed around, I was physically beat up, I was spit on, and I was kicked. I was bullied by my own family while I was down there. What did I learn from all of that?

I learned that sometimes your own family isn't thrilled to see you succeed.

I learned that just because everyone is with you, doesn't mean that they are for you. I learned that some people will come into your life for no other reason than for you to push them out of your life. I learned that you can be hated for being different. I learned that when things go wrong in life, simply telling someone about it with the expectation that they will help you is foolish. I learned that sometimes you have to endure hardship when you have no other options. I learned that life was neither fair nor rational.

So when you encounter these learning as I did in life; when and where no one is excited about your success—then you have to learn to be excited about it for yourself. I learned that there are people in this world who like nothing more than to watch from the sidelines until you succeed so that they can show up in your life to take from you what they did not help you get, but want for themselves.

I managed to survive the many fearful events of that week. As we got ready to leave, the pending bus trip looked like nirvana compared to what I'd just gone through. As much as had I told my Mom that I was being bullied and mistreated, she told me I was being a spoiled brat, to toughen up and stop exaggerating. That they were just playing. I guess persecution is in the eye of the beholder (or the persecuted). But it was terrible; terrible to the point where I said to my grandmother, with cousins and aunts and uncles listening on the day that we left, *"I will never come back here again, ever."* They laughed me off, but I meant it. That was thirty-one years ago. I have never been back to [Kentwood], Louisiana, and I do not have any plans to go back ... ever.

Four days later, we got back home to Providence. I got back to my life, got back to my private school, got back to my clothes I could actually wear and not have stolen. I got back to having a bathroom across the hall from my own bedroom—got back to not having to go out into the woods to relieve myself. I got back to my real world; I got back to my normal. And after a week, the frightening nightmares of that bus trip would end and I would finally get back to sleeping through the night without waking up crying.

I came back with a new appreciation for what I had ... and started to unconsciously form an idea of what were the things I wanted for my life. At eight years old, I had already seen what not seizing every opportunity for success would bring me. It was then and is to this day completely unacceptable to settle for less. I refuse to not live up to my potential. I knew at that young age who and what I never wanted to be ... like my "family" in Kentwood. Living up to my potential meant taking school seriously. I would heed my father's stern direction and focus. My time in Kentwood did have one positive effect on me. It introduced me to the importance of doing well in school if you want to succeed, and to my passion for life-long learning and personal growth.

* * *

I loved school, because school is where everything cool happened. Everything good, and fun, and exciting went on at school. My friends were at school. We had recess at school. We had all these different classes to take: art, gym. I loved school. I still love school to this day—not for the academic part of it, but more of the collegial aspect, the cohort aspect of being in a class of students, of people, of friends. A few of my first grade classmates are still my friends today. There's one woman I've known from the first grade. We probably lived about four blocks away from each other.

We would later go on to graduate from the same high school together. We're still friendly to this day. She has a beautiful family judging by the updates I see posted on Facebook. She was a friend, and someone whom to this day I think of as a sister. When I see her, I think instantly of my grade school years, having close friends, trading peanut butter and jelly sandwiches for ham sandwiches, playing chase at recess, going on field trips, visiting Rocky Point Park, and all those memorable childhood things from growing up in Providence.

At nine-years old, I realized from my other friends that they all spent time on the weekends with their fathers and their older or younger brothers doing great stuff. I didn't have that and wanted to have those memories. I remember talking to my Mom about it and saying, *"It'd be great if I had a big brother or somebody I could hang out with."* My Mom had heard from one of her friends about an organization called Big Brothers. She contacted Big Brothers of Rhode Island, and after a short interview about me, found out I met the qualifications or criteria to be a little brother. A few weeks later, I was matched with my first big brother.

As a result of that, from age nine through twelve I had three big brothers—all of which were college students in the Providence area. Two went to Brown University and one went to Johnson & Wales. I had three big brothers because each one was in their last years of college and would move from the Providence area after their graduation. It was a period of growth for me. I had a chance to meet and learn from these male role models—still young men themselves but older to me—who would take me out to a movie, spend time with me playing Frisbee or throwing the football around, take time to talk about the importance of going to college, and what I wanted to be when I grew up. I look back on that and those times fondly, and how those three gentlemen helped shape me. They took time out of their life for me—to spend time with me, two hours every other week. What did this collection of fond memories teach me?

They taught me about male bonding. They taught me that connecting with people on a deeper level is important for your growth and maturity. They taught me (reconfirmed really) how important it is to have a strong male presence in the life of a child. I matured quite a bit from age nine to twelve, because of those adult male interactions. My Mom was happy because I had proper male figures in my life. My Mom wasn't one of those women who had a stream of men coming in and out of her life or our house. If she did have a boyfriend during that time, it wasn't anybody I remember distinctly, because she had a lot of respect for me and for herself. So if she did have a boyfriend, it wasn't anybody she paraded in front of me as her son. I respect my mother so much to this day more than words can say for her discretion. She was indeed a woman, but she never once forgot that she was my Mom and a lady first.

* * *

At age 12 my Mom had already sent me to Catholic school for eight years and she was determined I go to a Catholic high school. This meant either a co-ed Catholic high school in Providence, which I really did not want to go to, because of all the different buses I'd have to take to get to it, or the all-boys Catholic high school way out (relative term) in Warwick that required a 40 minute drive in traffic. Actually, I just really didn't want to go to an all-boys school–period. While I didn't know what girls were all about then, I knew I liked having them around. I thought they made life funny and a little bit more interesting than just being around a bunch of dudes. I told my Mom I had a different choice. My Mom said, *"You will go to one of these two schools, or if you get accepted to Classical, you can go to there because it is a great school."* Classical High School in Providence was and is a college prep, charter high school. Many consider it to be the best public high school in the state of Rhode Island.

I took the entrance exams for each school and I got accepted into all three. I chose to go to Classical High School over La Salle Academy (a co-ed Catholic high school) and Bishop Hendricken (an all-boys Catholic high school). The other two schools were great institutions and I'd spend a lot of time around kids who went to La Salle and Hendricken in my high school years, as a student-athlete at Classical, but I didn't want to go to either one of them. I was fortunate enough to get into Classical, and that changed my life in a much different way. It gave me exposure to other kids, smart kids; kids from wealthy (comparatively) families who through my interactions with them, allowed me to see examples of my life and career aspirations of success. Through my friendships with these other kids, and time spent around their parents who treated me life one of their own sons, I gained a view of the world that I had never seen. These experiences gave me a reference for what it meant to be upper middle class and to be successful. I thankfully got to see the positive extreme of my harsh experiences in Kentwood many years earlier.

* * *

Back in 1986, almost everyone (even my rich kid friends on the East Side) who was twelve or thirteen had a job. One of the greatest gifts my Mom could have given me, in addition to a private school education, was getting me a job in with a local catering company. I'll never forget Driscoll and Lane Caterers. The Lane family owned a catering company that also had had a breakfast/lunch counter and corner store in my neighborhood. The Lanes were third-generation Irish-Catholics, solid people and hard workers in the restaurant business. Many families in the neighborhood loved them and were their customers. My Mom knew Steve, the older of two sons. To quiet my constant pestering, she talked to him and convinced him to give me my first real job. I was officially hired as a dishwasher working for minimum wage under the table on my thirteenth birthday ... and I couldn't be happier.

If you're asking, *"How does your Mom getting you a job equate to a great gift?"* Well, my Mom gifted me my first instance of independence when I got that job as a dishwasher at age thirteen. My first job in life making $3.15 an hour; in two hours, I got more than I'd ever received from her as an allowance for a week. The important thing was that I was getting paid. I would go after school and I'd sweep and mop the floors with a smile. On the weekends I'd scrub pots and pans and grin.

I'd get paid every week, come home and give my Mom some of that money. She never asked for it, but I just did. I felt like I should do it—because, if you'll remember, I was mirroring what my father had done. When you get your paycheck, you come home and you throw it on the table and give some to Mom. I kept doing that. I was following the example. But with the rest of the money, I did what my Mom did. I'd go to the Old Stone Bank and put that money away. *Yabba dabba do!* I kept doing it, making my money, giving Mom some and saving the rest in my own bank account. I worked the remainder of the school year for Driscoll and Lane Caterers, and made a bunch of money. Of course, bunch is a relative term. What I will say is that this was the most money I had seen since the days when Pop would dump his loot on the kitchen table. I would work for Driscoll and Lane until the summer after my senior year of high school. Those paychecks would pay for my school clothes, my spending money, my car, my car insurance, oil changes, and gasoline while at Classical.

My first job taught me what it meant to work, what it meant to save your money for the things you want. It taught me everybody has to do their part. Nothing comes easy. Nothing is given to you. You have to work for everything. That is the work ethic I learned as a black teenager working for a third-generation Irish-Catholic immigrant family who owned their own business and only knew their success was due to their value placed on hard work. I learned more, and enjoyed working more for Steve Lane, than from any other boss I've had in my career. From him I learned what it meant to really work. What it meant to sweat to get something done. I knew what it meant to ask for help instead of quitting if things got tough. I knew what it meant to get down on your hands and knees to scrub the kitchen floor to make the place clean. I learned to have pride in your work effort, pride in your performance, and the benefits of paying exacting attention to detail.

There were these two magical phrases Steve used— to this day they are stuck in my mind. When I would wash dishes, he would tell me, *"Every pot, every pan, every dish, every spoon, every fork has a front and a back. Make sure you wash both. You have to make it shine.* From this exchange came the first magical phrase: *If it's mine, you'd better make it shine."* I thought that was interesting. He wasn't being possessive or domineering. He was talking about it from the standpoint of having pride in your work. Don't just wash the inside of the pot; wash the outside, too. He taught me about attention to detail, how to be meticulous in what you're doing—especially when you are paid to do them. That is a basic, but important lesson that I have applied to my career philosophy as well.

Another of his viewpoints was comical. Steve was a guy who really expected you to work for your money. If he was paying you for the hour, he wanted his money worth for that hour. He wasn't mean about it, but you knew he was serious. One day he caught me leaning against the wall. Just leaning and watching the TV that was on in the kitchen. He saw me and didn't say anything at first. Of course, I was too young to realize I probably shouldn't have been leaning like that. After what must have been too long of a break, he came over he looked at me, and said, *"Does the place look clean to you?"* I said, *"Yeah, I think it looks pretty clean."* He asks, *"What about behind the stove?"* I replied, *"I've never cleaned back there."* He then shared the second magic phrase: *"If you've got time to lean, you've got time to clean."* Shocked, I said *"What?"* He clarified his statement, *"If you've got time to stand around and lean and get paid for it, you've got time to clean. So, let's get behind that stove. In fact, let's take apart and clean the stove piece by piece."*

He taught me right there the difference, between being finished and being done. I then didn't know what that meant. Finished means are you all set for today. Done means you've done everything that needs to, and can be done. You have cleaned everything that needs to be cleaned, where you can run a white cloth napkin under a counter edge and not see a speck of dirt or filth on the cloth. I worked so hard to clean the place that some days Steve had to tell me to go home. He never balked at paying me the overtime. He paid me to do work. I wanted to get to done ... even to this day; I don't believe there is such a thing in life as done. Not to wax religiously here, but I think that not even in death will you be done ... you will just be finished with this life. My faith tells me that there is more yet to come.

I remember getting what was a big check for a young kid back then. I had worked an 80-hour week and when you think about being a thirteen-year old working an 80-hour week, that's beyond crazy! But I did—I would get up in the morning and get to work at six, and I'd stay until ten o'clock at night. Work had become my friend, and working hard had become my passion.

In that one 80-hour week I made that kitchen spotless. It was July, so while my friends were at the beach playing in the sand, I was sweeping up sand from in front of the Driscoll and Lane corner store. I was on ladders washing walls, I was under tables, I was mopping floors, and I cleaned the cellar walk in refrigerators. I did it all. I wanted to see what done felt like. He never told me to do all those things. I cleaned that whole place... spotless. I worked so hard that Steve gave me so much money at the end of the week in my paycheck that he said, "*You know what? Don't come back next week.*" I thought I was fired, or at least no longer needed. I replied, "*Steve, I'm leaving the week after next on vacation to Virginia with my Mom.*" He said, "*Even better. Enjoy your vacation. I'll see you when you get back.*" I then realized what done meant. I had cleaned his place from top to bottom. He told me, "*My place hasn't been this clean since we opened it. Thank you.* In later years, we'd laugh about how hard I worked that week. But to get paid for that 80-hour week was ridiculous. I took my cash money, went home, and threw it on the table to show to my Mom that her son could do the same thing too. The next morning, I went straight to Old Stone Bank the next day to make a deposit in my own account. I was doing what both my Mom and my Pop taught me to do.

What did working this 80-hour week teach me? It taught me that if I put my mind to any seemingly impossible professional task, I could meet it head up and eyes open. I learned that the one thing you cannot do to me is tell me that I cannot do something. I learned that only I could stand in the way of my own success. And I learned that my failures in life would only leave me with myself to blame for not trying harder, or finding another way to get something done.

When work was finished each day, I could literally walk right down the street (across a major street) from work to my home—a three block walk. I would call my Mom and say, *"I'm leaving now,"* and Steve would take the phone and say, *"Okay, he's walking out now"* and they'd stay on the phone until I got home. That was of course my Mom's time to find out from my boss how I was doing at work. I'd try to beat my record of how long it took me to get from Steve Lane's door to my Mom's door. I ran the whole way and had it down to a science. The fastest I ever got there was three minutes and thirteen seconds and that's including waiting for traffic to clear on either side of the street. Granted, I probably could have gone a little faster, but after working fifteen, sixteen hours, that was about as fast as I could go that late in the evening.

In the span of time working at my first job I learned a lot of lessons from many people ... but mostly I learned a lot about myself. And that "Steve Lane" work ethic has served as my foundation and factored greatly in how I approach work and success in my life. When my work becomes mundane or I feel less than challenged, when I feel myself figuratively leaning against that wall again in Steve's kitchen, I find something else to do. I challenge myself instead of waiting for someone else to challenge me or keep me engaged.

STUCK IN THE MIDDLE

In the following chapters you'll see that the early challenges I worked through as a boy and what I discovered about myself through self-discovery as a young man, formed my professional philosophy and how I approach my career. In these next chapters, you will see first-hand how I used these early learned experiences to escape being stuck in the middle.

CHAPTER TWO

You can't pay the bills without being happy

Action may not always bring happiness; but there is no happiness without action.

– Benjamin Disraeli

I had someone tell me not very long ago *"You can't pay your bills without being happy."* I thought that was pretty interesting in the context of the conversation I was having with this colleague of mine. We talked about observing people in airports flying to and fro. I call them the Blue Blazer Society. They appear to be Baby Boomer generation men running around wearing blue blazers, with a light blue button down collared shirt underneath, khaki or gray pants, and loafers ... were they selling things, traveling to meetings, or headed to a convention? And I would sit and wonder, are they happy? Are these busy folks really happy? Many of them seem to be well paid, "Executive Land" types but if you look closely they don't appear happy. They don't appear like they're enjoying where they are going or what they're doing. I've felt it myself and wondered some days, *"Am I really enjoying my job?"* or *"Do I really want to be here?"*

What's interesting is that I actually started to believe that being happy in your career and work didn't really matter. You can pay the bills without being happy it seemed. But I would later realize for myself once and for all that this anecdote really meant that you can't be unhappy with what you do for work, and smile as you pay your bills. I decided there and then that I would not continue working to make someone else successful at the expense of what made me happy. So I took charge of finding my true career happiness. And since then, paying my bills became not only easier but some days became downright enjoyable and satisfying.

There are a lot of unhappy Gen Xers out there who are not making the money they need to live the life they want to live, should live, or feel they could live—because they're trying to pay the bills without being happy. What does that mean for the Gen Xer who is stuck in the middle? I think that's one of the hardest pills to for my generation to swallow, the fact of we are seeking career happiness, equilibrium, balance, and we are quickly coming to the realization we can't pay our bills and don't want to live our lives without being happy. We're trading career happiness for money to be able to live a better life, but are instead slowly living a life much like our Baby Boomer coworkers and bosses. It's an interesting juxtaposition in the form of a steep climb of the personal career decision tree with branches are so twisted it is hard to determine which limb to choose that will allow us to reach the blue sky.

That's very important because that's what I've experienced in "Executive Land." You almost have to become a different person to be an executive. For some Gen Xers, that process doesn't really fit them. It's hard to turn off who you are each day, or not be the person who you have been up this point in life just for the sake of making a certain amount of money or for the sake of having a certain title.

As a Gen Xer, the sad truth is that you've got to do your time or prove yourself in the company before you're taken seriously or for the Baby Boomers to see you as the executive you know yourself to be capable of becoming. Everyone will tell you that there's no greater way to prove yourself in any company than to deliver well on products with consistency. We all get paid to do things for an organization. There's a clever little sentence that's tacked onto every job description that's ever been created: "... *and other duties as assigned.*" Organizations use this catch phrase as a get out of jail free card to ask employees to deliver on things that have not been thought of yet.

Proving yourself in every company is different. Some organizations want you to deliver on creating a strategy to save money or make money. Others will say delivering is simply adding to the value of the company, still other will expect strategic thinking and tactical doing. Some might believe that delivering is leading and managing.

Those two distinctly different things though they are often lumped together. I believe you lead people but you manage projects. As an executive, I didn't manage my people, I led them and allowed them to amaze me with the things they could do. One of my favorite things to say to my direct reports was,

"I'll tell you what, why, and when ... You get to amaze me with how."

I don't like to tell people how to do their job because I don't like people telling me how to do my job. If you hire someone to tell them how to do their job, why don't you just do the job yourself and save someone the misery of micromanagement. So I instead, I just want to tell them what they need to do and allow them to use their creativity, their intellect, their professionalism, and their expertise to come back with an innovative solution to the needs as presented.

As I found myself moving farther up the ladder, you would think that leading would be the skill that I would be measured on most often, but in "Executive Land", it can be difficult to find that right mix of delivery, of owning things—not only from a tactical standpoint but from a strategic one as well. I think many of my Gen X counterparts struggle with that as well, because we have Baby Boomer bosses, who do not believe we should be here yet. They still see you as a kid, and say, *"Okay, kid, go work on this."* They don't welcome us at the strategy table yet because they don't believe our "youthful" career trajectory allows us to be at the table to share in the strategic thought generation. That's probably one of the biggest mistakes the Baby Boomer leaders make is thinking that only their generation has any strategic thinking to add at the table.

Unfortunately, that's going to come back to bite a lot of them in the pants. My generation of colleagues realizes the fact that we're worth a lot more than we're getting credit for, and that's why we're stuck in the middle. We're stuck between the two generations and trying to prove ourselves to both. Trying to prove that we can and should be where we are—sadly it seems to a bunch of people who could care less that we're there. Keep in mind the image from our earlier look at our current position in the generational career traffic jam.

How do you remain visible in a place where many would rather stick you somewhere so you'll be invisible? That's something we'll expand on in this book. There is a lot of value Gen Xers could add, more that we can do, but we're not getting a chance to make those contributions. That feeling of being undervalued, underestimated, and marginalized contributes to the purported Generation X malaise and why many of us now know that you can't really pay your bills without being happy.

CHAPTER THREE

Selling Yourself in the Real World
(and the push back you might encounter)

There are two kinds of people, those who do the work and those who take the credit. Try to be in the first group; there is less competition there.

— Indira Gandhi

There is an initial transaction between someone applying for a position and their prospective employer (the company looking to fill a position). And it involves something that many Gen Xers are uncomfortable with but exists in the job market (and in their career climb) and that is the need to know how to position and present yourself, i.e. sell yourself. This is especially important in today's recession wracked business environment.

The best way to sell yourself is by being prepared—and in many ways by doing this—it does the selling for you. It's self-promotion by preparation. That's one of the key things I share with those who ask my for career advice. You can do it. And by doing it you start down a path to lead you to what you want. This simple effort separates the men from the boys and the women from the girls.

If you know the role you want, and you've looked at all that you have to do, or the experiences you need to have, and said, *"That's too hard, will take too long, or I don't want to do it."* You just told yourself everything you need to know about yourself. You know now that you really don't want it bad enough. You want the trappings, you want the rewards, you want the glory ... but you aren't prepared to do the work it takes to get there. And you know what? That's not a comfortable conversation for someone to have with themselves, but it's one of the most necessary conversations you will ever have in your career. It's easier to get somewhere in life and career if you are brutally honest enough to understand who and where you are from the beginning. If you don't feel like you're ready or don't want to do all that it would take to reach your aspirations, then don't do it. But more importantly, don't whine, cry, and moan to all who will listen when you don't get to that level if you know deep down in your heart that you haven't done everything or are not willing to do everything it takes to succeed.

To reach executive management we're not simply talking about entering a popularity contest. Yes, popularity and professional brand are important, but at the end of the day, it all boils down to the resume you place in front of the hiring manager and how you come across as the embodiment of those credentials on paper.

What about your resume stands out? What does your resume lack?

One goal I have for myself that I will share with you is this. I've always set myself up so that whenever my resume is put in the hands of a decision maker, for the position I know I am ready for, I never want them to think, *"This guy would be perfect for us if he only had _____."*

I've been obsessive in my work on taking care so that never happens. There is no *"if only he had"* to be found in reading my resume. Perhaps that strategy could work for you too. Ask for feedback on your resume from others; address any misses they find in your resume by filling them with either new experiences or learning where appropriate. I don't believe you can be overqualified. Overqualified is not in my vocabulary. I prefer highly qualified. Highly qualified says I am versatile and have many transferable skills, whereas overqualified says I am at the end of the line in one job or career field.

I studied my resume long and hard. And then, I went shopping. I went online and found job descriptions for the roles I would want to have, and printed out the job descriptions. Everything I saw as a required, or a recommended skill in those job descriptions, I put on a qualifications shopping list. When I had a full list of what I felt I needed to have, I went about getting those experiences, the correct level of education, and the most contemporary certifications. What do I need to have on my resume that is currently missing but is recommended, or needed for the role I'm looking for with a good company? Better yet, what things should be on my resume that will make them think, *"We have to talk to this this guy ... his background and experience is perfect for this position."*

I have worked in multiple industries at increasing levels of accountability and seniority, building my career step-by-step. I have been an entrepreneur. I have built and sold a business. I have a doctorate in education. I've worked for international companies. I'm certified in HR. I'm certified in project management. I have been a Vice President. I am a military veteran. I have and interesting story to tell. I am good at connecting with people.

In short, I worked hard to make myself into the perfect candidate. It's taken a lot of sacrifice, time, and plenty of money to be able to do that, but I believe that if you're going to compete for the top positions, you've got to be exemplary, you've got to be extraordinary, and a lot of hard work goes into that. Not only in establishing the strength of the resume, and credentials but also in networking to make the right contacts that will help you in your career. I never lost site of the fact that the resume I have built is only to get me the interview. It is up to me once I am in the interview to know and sell myself so well, that I get the job. I have been smart enough to never turn down an interview, and wise enough to not accept every job offer. This position of strength plays into the many things I will share with you.

I'll share more about owning your own succession plan. I'll share more about reverse engineering the role by looking at the job descriptions of today that you want to be in tomorrow. I'll share more about strengthening your resume to better sell yourself and the importance of planning your own professional development from now on. I'll share more about things I've learned the hard way. I will share things that organizations can do differently with regard to talent management, employee engagement, talent acquisition and talent retention.

I have experienced, as mentioned earlier, the cold hard reality that that not everybody wants to see you succeed. That's probably one of the hardest things to discover for my Gen Xer colleagues. By my nature, I'm a very open and sharing type of person. And while this sometimes comes back to bite me hard, I'll help anyone. I'm always proud to see somebody succeed. I'm always happy for them when I hear that somebody's gotten the job they wanted. But not everybody is enthusiastic or happy to see you succeed. I am convinced that some people live in this world just to see others fail. And if you are not expecting to encounter this—when you do—it can be a bit demoralizing at first and more than a little frustrating.

There are a wealth of personal experiences I have had as a Gen Xer that serve as reasons for me to feel this way. In my positions with companies most of the people I worked with were older than me. I was younger than most of my direct reports. My peers were at least four to five years older than me. My bosses were all at least fifteen years my senior. Many of them thought I came out of nowhere: Who is this thirty-something year old kid, and where did he come from? How did he get to where we are so quickly? What did he do that was different than what we did? How can we slow him down so he doesn't pass me or show me up? How can I get him out of the organization as soon as possible? How can I instead of helping him acclimate to the culture here, advertise his missteps so that I can look good?

How then did I walk through this minefield of contempt?

I followed the very advice, and used the same logic I'm offering in this book.

Allow my arrogance to come through, if it has not already to this point. Many times in my career, I'm seated at a table in a conference room with peers who have spent a greater number of years in their career to get to their positions. They were older than me, had been at it longer than me, and yet there I was at the same place ... earlier, faster, sharper, and with more demonstrated success than they had to date. It rubbed them the wrong way; and I knew it did. Some of them have even said, *"You intimidate people."* Or they give me my personal favorite ... *"You have a strong presence."* Of course I have a presence. I am unlike anyone they know who looks like me. I know that my physical size, darker skin tone, relative youth, high level of education, deep work experience, veteran status, self-confidence to the point of arrogance, ability to self-promote, ease of networking, booming voice, and sense of humor scared them professionally, and quite likely frightened some of them personally.

You know what? That is who I am. That is the person you hired. I am comfortable with being my authentic self. I can't control what people think or do. I can't control when people dump hate on me or other people because I have achieved what they (A) want to achieve and never will, or (B) have achieved the same success in record time compared to them.

These are some of the things you deal with as you move up the ladder—it's the pushback you might receive if you dare to be your authentic self. Especially as a Gen Xer, when you've got Baby Boomers sitting in the same seats in the same meetings around the table with you, and they are shocked at how you made it. It's not so much where you are right now that concerns them. It is often because they come face to face with who they wish they were personally or where they wish they were in their career. They realize that you will surpass them and will be and do more than they have done in their career. That pisses off the people mentioned above. It's interesting to watch how things go on in this world of work. Not everyone wants to see you be there in that room, or at that table.

And you will certainly encounter people like that—chances are good they will be your peers, and may even be your own boss. They are not necessarily going to publically hold you down, but they may work behind the scenes to slow you down, or flatten your career trajectory. Because they believe you should "do your time." Probably the worst thing you can say to a Gen Xer, *"I know you think you're ready, but you haven't been here long enough. You haven't done this long enough."* To say to a Gen Xer who is highly qualified, and highly motivated that you haven't been here long enough to be qualified? That's one of the most demoralizing things you could say to someone. For me, that is right up there with, *"you have to earn my trust."* I hate that expression because it is as counter-cultural and foreign to me as a Gen Xer to have somebody say, *"Look, you've got to earn my trust."* I am the opposite. I believe you should give people your trust. Then they have responsibility for maintaining it up front, and then the only thing they can do is lose that trust. I give my trust freely. I will trust someone until I realize they are trying to screw me by using that trust to upstage me for their gain, or in some other way violate that trust, and then I start to pull it back.

The counter to the pushback you will encounter is to continue to focus and deliver on the attributes and opportunities that initially got you to the table. An intelligent approach to using the tools in your career toolbox, rational decision making, taking calculated career risks, strategic networking, and owning your own succession plan by making achieving your career aspirations a personal and professional habit.

How do you own your own succession plan you might ask? We'll talk about that in the next chapter.

CHAPTER FOUR

Owning Your Own Plan (A Three-Year Strategy)

Don't limit yourself. Many people limit themselves to what they think they can do. You can go as far as you mind lets you. What you believe, you can achieve.

— **Mary Kay Ash**

You own your own succession plan.

I've said this to many of my fellow Gen Xers that I've coached and mentored. You can't wait for an organization to see you as being a high potential or that you are an up-and-comer before you take advantage of doing things for your own career.

Most of us who are Gen Xers in the workforce grew up being raised by parents who were traditionalists or early Baby Boomers. Their counsel to us was find a great company out of college, go there, work really hard, and apply yourself, make yourself indispensable, and you'll move up in the company. You will have a career path, you'll be on your way to making a great salary, having a retirement plan, and everything else will take care of itself.

That's what we were told growing up, but we later discovered a cruel irony.

Many Gen Xers instead watched their parents and older family members spend years in an organization—20, 30, or 40 years— only to end up being let go, laid off, downsized, or right-sized ... just before the dream of a grand retirement, and the gold watch came to fruition. And for some, their layoff was simply to save the company long-term money by not having to pay another retiree's medical benefits or retirement paycheck. The cruel irony is that after giving your working life to the company, just when you need the company the most... is when they no longer want or care about you. What we were told and believed just didn't happen. And, I don't think those days of trust are ever going to come back again.

The era of corporate loyalty to employees is over.

The reality is today when you go into an organization, you're an at-will employee. They know it, and you should never forget it. Loyalty is now most often a word spoken of only in relation to customers of the company and not of the company to the employees. Many Gen Xers realize they can be let go at any time for anything. That's what at-will means. No loyalty to employees, and no "good-faith clause" between you and your employer. Your relationship to the company is purely transactional. As long as you fit into their plans or into the current economic conditions for the business—then you'll have a job. The minute something in that changes—you may find you're out of a job.

Uncertainty makes owning your own succession plan a career imperative.

You have to know what you want to do, who you want to be, where you want to go. The most important thing is when you go into any organization, you don't change your overall goal or dream of whom or what you want to become—that must be rock solid at all times. As for Gen Xers, many of us view the organization as just a means to get us to where we want to go. At the earliest indication that our time or role with the organization will no longer move us toward our career goals—

we will look for opportunities elsewhere with another organization.

How you continue to move toward preparing yourself to reach your professional and career goals is by owning your own succession plan.

I think about what this has meant for my own career.

First and foremost, was my succession plan focused on making Vice President at a Fortune 100 company by the time I turned 40. I figured if I could make Vice President by age 40, and Senior Vice President by age 50–that would give me a good, solid ten years as the Chief Learning Officer or Chief Talent Officer, to do great things for the company, be proud of my accomplishments, and subsequently retire with a solid 401k and a lot of deferred compensation; still young enough to enjoy a life away from the corporate grind.

I worked hard for ten years to make Vice President and made it early; eighteen months before turning 40. But as I went hard after my goal, some days I would wonder if that was what I really wanted to do. While deep down I still had the aspiration of one day becoming a Chief Learning Officer, or Chief Talent Officer, the end of the ten-year race to VP taught me deep personal lessons and allowed me to rediscover my career passion. As such, my career has taken an exciting detour and allowed me to embrace my rediscovered passion for being an entrepreneur. The first showing of that passion is the book you are currently reading.

One of the leaders I'm fortunate enough to have had a conversation with in my previous job said to me, *"the higher you go up, the more you give up."* That's an interesting observation. Think about the impact of that simple truth. (It gave me pause.) It was like a splash of cold water in the face.

The higher you go, the more you give up. He talked about it very openly. He talked about giving up time with his wife and his family to get to the level where he was the head of HR for a Fortune 100 company.

He had to make deep career trades.

He had to make serious personal and family sacrifices.

And he had to ask for trades and sacrifices to also be made by family to enable to him to get to that position.

I wondered if I really wanted to do that.

Is that senior executive role at a Fortune 100 company, if it were one day offered to me, something I will really feel so strongly about that I would, at that time, again be willing to give up things to move higher up?

I am not sure, but I do know enough to never say never. So the jury is still out for me. But the jury may come back with a verdict for you by the time you finish this book. I think it's important to give you a complete perspective on this from someone who has lived it, and is reporting on what it is like to pursue the corporate dream and has attained the professional career goal of making it to the executive level with a major company.

Owning your succession plan is figuring out who you want to be, and going after it.

There was a movie a few years ago called *The Pursuit of Happyness* with Will Smith that has really stuck in my mind as it relates to this discussion. In the movie, Will Smith portrays Chris Gardner. Gardner had invested heavily in a device known as a "Bone Density Scanner". He felt like he had it made selling these devices. However, they did not sell as they were marginally better than the current technology but at a much higher price. As Gardner tried to figure out how to sell them, his wife left him; he lost his house, his bank account, and credit cards. Forced to live on the streets with his son, Gardner was now desperate to find a steady job. The most fascinating scene in the movie begins with him walking down a street (presumably in the Wall Street area of New York). He had had a hard day trying to sell the Bone Density Scanners to doctors' offices and hospitals to make money to feed his family. As he walked, he saw a well-dressed man, getting out of a red Ferrari in front of a building. Gardner smiled, and said to the guy "I have just two questions for you: *What do you do, and how do you do it?"* He is amazed to learn that this guy is a stockbroker. And even more amazing to him, is that in a quick conversation with the guy, learns that you don't need to go to college to become a stockbroker ... you just need to be good with numbers, and good with people. After the guy exchanges a couple of quick words and a joke with Gardner, he entered a building. On the sidewalk, as Gardner looked around, he notices how happy everyone seems. Struck by how everyone coming and going was smiling it is at that movement he began his pursuit of "happyness" and took on a job as a stockbroker. But before he could receive pay, he needed to go through six months of make or break training. He also needed to sell the rest of his Bone Density Scanners.

That one scene would be how I would approach my career going forward.

I see the conversation with the stockbroker in the movie as a model that anyone could follow for themselves. This conversation is something anybody can have for their career (and their personal life) with someone who is doing what you want to do. All you have to do, when you see somebody doing what you want to do, or who has what you want—whether it's the right car, the right job, the right house—is have the courage and the conviction to ask them, *"Can you tell me what you do and how you do it?"* I would suggest that you wouldn't come across to them as intrusive. Most successful people will answer you. They may not go item-by-item and tell you how to conduct your own life or a map how to live it, but they may tell you what they did, and then you can take that information and fashion it into a career toolbox shopping list that you can use to better build your career and actually own your own succession plan.

That is what I have done and it has paid dividends above my expectations.

I looked at leaders who were in the roles I aspired to—Chief Learning Office or Chief Talent Officer—and I looked at their resumes and bios, their experiences and what they've done. Almost all of them were either Ph.D. or Ed.D. or they had a JD. They were very young for the position. They had a meteoric rise through the ranks of not just one organization but others as well. They took risks by moving from company to company, and from state to state; some took international assignments. All of them have continued to progress and move forward in their profession by speaking at conferences, and writing books or articles. They all worked hard growing their brand through networking, and making time to connect with other people in their field. They work to meet people who are in the roles they one day want to have for themselves. They were very focused in their pursuit of the next level of their professional career.

I studied them and what they'd done to get to where they were and I thought deeply about it. I planned for how I could put myself in those situations where:

(A) I could network both internally and externally to the company

(B) I could meet people who held the roles I aspired to hold

(C) I could learn to speak their language

(D) I could write articles or a book where my voice could contribute to my profession

I started looking at where these people congregated and at what time. Are there societies or groups they are a member of professionally? Is there a meeting or networking event that they all go to each week, month, or quarter? If there were conferences they went to once a year, I would go to those conferences. I asked around to learn where I should go to get better connected to these and other career role models. Where ever I needed to be, I tried hard to be at the right place and time. If there were magazines I should be reading, I would subscribe to them. If there are blogs I should be reading, I started reading them.

I worked hard on my LinkedIn profile to where people can see my credentials, see who I am connected with, and look at my background. I am very selective about who I connect with on LinkedIn, because my networking brand is important to me. None of the professionals in my network are there just because their background looks cool—that's just not how I prefer to network—I intentionally only link to or accept link requests from people I know personally, have worked with in the past, or where we both belong to the same professional association. I see this as a necessary prerequisite to linking to someone and a condition to have them (as I am for them) as part of my network for shared career and professional exposure.

Here is in my opinion probably one of the best exercises anyone can do.

Reverse engineer job postings that are a match for your career aspirations.

This is common sense to me but that's because I've spent so much time trying to make the system work for me and how to get ahead as fast, as far, and as quickly as I could.

For example, I often searched for Vice President, Learning and Development, or Vice President, Talent Management job descriptions. When I would find them, I would cut and paste the text from those job descriptions into a Word document or save it as a PDF file because I was not yet applying for those jobs. My plan and thinking was to make sure I had a comprehensive reference library of the skills to use in taking charge of my own succession plan. I wanted to be sure that I was setting myself up to have the right set of credentials to support my candidacy when it came time for me to actually apply for those positions.

Work on having the complete toolbox they want in the perfect candidate.

I said to myself, *"I want that job in ten years"* and took job descriptions for the positions I wanted to have and saved them to a file I created for myself and labeled it as "My Resume Shopping List" I combed over every open Vice President, Talent of Management posting, and every Vice President, Learning and Development job out there. I researched and documented what the commonalities were in each. The first was they want you to have certification—either HR or project management. That was a common thread. So I chose achieving those two certifications as my first goal.

In June 2006, I got certified in project management. I studied hard and came back in August of 2006 and got certified in human resources. Check the box on both of those.

Another thread I noticed was that they all asked for the candidate to have at least a Master's degree; some positions preferred that the candidate have a Doctorate. So I went after obtaining a doctorate since I already had a Master's degree. I started a doctoral program at Pepperdine University in Malibu, California in July of 2005 and finished in June of 2009. Check the box on that preference/requirement and add it to the toolbox.

Many job descriptions asked that the candidate have worked for a Fortune 100 company. So I targeted and was lucky enough to find my way into MetLife, and Comcast, which are definitely very large, well-known organizations. Both are in the Fortune 100. Check the box on those nice/need to have experience. Realizing that the job you want is out there but that you may not be ready yet can be a motivating force to get ready. Resist being frustrated or just throwing your resume out there everywhere and thinking, *"I hope to somebody will give me a shot even though I know I am not 100% what they need." "I hope someone will grow me into being their candidate of choice."* That will not bring you closer to an opportunity, and it may even push one out of reach.

Resist that urge to force an opportunity if you know you are not ready for it.

I spent ten years working at and figuring out how to optimize my approach and myself for the job market targeting an eventual climb to the executive level in a large company.

The day I walked out of the Navy in August 2000, I said to myself, *"I want to make VP by the time I'm 40, and I want my career to be in learning and development."* That started my movement forward, and drove me to put my own succession plan in place. I told myself,

"By the end of ten years, I want to have all the experiences that will allow me to apply for any one of these Vice President level jobs and at least get the interview, and go in confidently in knowing that I had built up the personal and professional interviewing skills to land the job."

Many Gen Xers realize your resume only gets you the interview. However, many do not act with the realization that it is the interview that gets you the job.

It's not good enough to have a great resume if you can't sell yourself.

You have to be able to sell yourself as the embodiment of the resume. You need to build experience to handle any question that comes to you in the interview. You have to have a plan. I have approached each job I have had with what I call my "Three-Year Plan". When other employers and other Gen Xers hear that they ask, *"What do you mean? You mean you're only going to be here (at this job, in this role) for three years?"* It could sound that way to some but my plan is simply stated.

I never plan to stay with any organization more than three years.

If I do, then that's great, but I never expect to be there that long. I never go somewhere and say, *"I'm going to stay for the next 20 years."* I think that's ridiculous, because the organization you join today, something could happen or change, beyond your control and it would not be the same organization tomorrow. Just look at what's taken place in many industries and with many companies in the past few years to see this is true. It will be even more prevalent in the future as companies seek maximum flexibility (which is often at a cost to employees) to respond to changes in the business and economic environment. It's happened to me a few times in my career. I've gone to work for this great place with a great boss and the next thing I know, the organization has some sort of leadership change or something happens and makes the great place where I started to work … become not such a great place to stick around.

Three-Year Plan: Year One

Figure out the organization. Look at, listen to, and learn from everyone. Organizations have an overall personality, a culture, if you will, just like people. It's important to get a feel for that so that you can see how you fit within that framework. You work hard. You try to meet people, network, grow your brand, handle some projects and have some wins. Be seen as a team player and someone who can be counted on.

One method I have found that works in this paradigm is an adaptation of Michael Watkins' book, *The First 90 Days*. It's a great book and I even consider myself a bit of a disciple of the book. It is within that first 90 days, where I found my own onboarding model that works for me. I think it's something that has helped me to move things forward in my own career. This little change in thinking may also help you.

The first 90 days is constructed of three, 30-day periods. The first 30 days is all about <u>discovery</u>. It too is all about look, listen, and learn. The next 30 days is about picking a particular thing to act on—whether it's a task or a project—and working that thing to the bone by under promising and really over <u>delivering</u> on it. The third 30 days, you <u>evaluate</u>, do you your lessons learned, and you piece together what you'll be able to share out as a direct result of the actions you've taken. I call my onboarding plan "DDE" as a mnemonic reminder for the three steps of Discovery, Delivery, and Evaluation.

It may seem simplistic, but I think the first year with an organization is made up of multiple ninety-day sprints, stops and starts. You go through discovery, delivery, and evaluation every ninety days to ensure that you are adding value to your organization. You ensure that you are adding to the fabric of the company. Your year one in an organization and in these 90-day cycles that make it up are really about trying to figure out how did my efforts make an impact, what did I do during this time, and how is the organization better for me having done this, or from me focusing my time and effort here?

If we do those things and we work hard like that, ramp up time in an organization flies by. It will keep you engaged. It helps you do what you need to do, which is succeed. That's a parallel to how I've built my life and career—through constant personal and professional discovery, delivery, and evaluation.

Three-Year Plan: Year Two

Now it's time to deliver, deliver, and deliver. Everything you put your name on, you have to do your best to make sure it is a solid deliverable, a solid product. You want people to say, "Wow, s/he did this, s/he did a fantastic job." Year two is all about delivering on your work, delivering on promises and delivering on relationships. Doing things in a way where you are actually known for owning something for the company. Something or some task that you put your name on it, and build a strong brand based on having done something significant for the organization.

Delivering over and over again by now has to have become a habit for you. If not, go back to discovery quickly because you may not have looked, listened, or learned thoroughly enough the first time.

Three-Year Plan: Year Three

It's all about evaluation. Evaluating the work you've done, evaluating the relationships you've created, evaluating whether or not you think you're going to have a future with the organization—and the last step is the most important part. Assessing what's next for you with the company and whether or not you have a future if you remain. This conversation with yourself should start halfway through year three. By the time year three arrives, you should have worked hard to be known to the organization and to know the organization. You've delivered, you've gotten some notice and you've built the foundation, a brand that's always at the top of your game.

You must also appraise how those things you've done have impacted the business, for the better—bringing about noticeable change in behavior, growth of revenue, saving of dollars, something of that nature—tangible evidence of your benefit to the organization. As you go through this period of evaluation, ask yourself, "Do I have a future with this organization? Will this organization sustain my career growth? Is there a true career path here for me? And you need to confirm that with your boss in the organization—to be sure that s/he sees things the same way as you do. If what you and s/he believe is positive about your place and future prospects in the organization you can then reset your three-year clock. That's what I do if it looks like the situation is working for me ... I plan for another three year stint.

As a Gen Xer, I've only been with one company for a full three years, not including my ten years with the Navy. I think that's pretty telling from the standpoint that even with my three-year plan, I've only been able to get from one company what I wanted in those three years. You might ask why? Simple, I was on this mission. I was on a personal fast track to my goal of Vice President. I did not have time to waste. I would not stay with any company where there were too many layers, a heavy bureaucracy, or the "you've got to be here for a long time before we'll trust you" and "you've got to be here for a long time before you move up" sentiment I mentioned previously. Even with the company where I was hired as a Vice President, I only made it through year one before I realized my career passions had changed along the way in completing that ten-year journey.

As I mentioned previously, I did work for one employer for three years. I enjoyed my time there and executed my three-year plan. I had delivered and was evaluated to have had positive results from my peers and boss and got to the place where I said, "I am ready for the next level". At the time, I was a director. I mentioned to my boss in my annual performance review, "I am interested in making Assistant Vice President." I was however told, "Most employees who make Assistant Vice President have to be a Director for at least eight to ten years." I was shocked. You've got to be kidding me. I've just had three stellar years, my evaluations had proven that, but I wasn't even going to be given a scratch at becoming an Assistant Vice President for another five years?

That just rubbed me the wrong way. So, at three years, I took my exit. I was lucky enough to have an opportunity present itself to me that was more in line with my goals and I ran with it. The other organization said, "We like your knowledge, skills, and abilities. We would like to have you work with us. For this position, you'll be promoted, you will move up now. You'll get promoted and you'll do more of what you want to do and are passionate about doing." And that decision to own my own succession plan and take my leave has paid dividends. It's allowed me to get to the place I wanted to get to in record time compared to many others.

Of course, this success comes with challenges and sacrifices but, as I said earlier, if you're not willing to put forth the effort (and make some sacrifices) ... then you really don't want personal success that badly yet.

My three-year plan is something a lot of Baby Boomers may find to be odd, but to a Gen Xer it may not sound strange at all. As Gen Xers most of us only stay with a company for three to five years anyway. Those who stay with a company for five years, many do so only because at five years they are vested in their 401k, and in their restricted stock as part of their package of benefits. That's great and all, but I don't think you should let a great opportunity go by because you are waiting around for vesting. Some Gen Xers might think I am crazy. Folks like Suze Orman might say, *"That's free money. At least stay long enough to take it with you."* I look at it like this, and this might be another generational nod to being a Gen Xer: I say you can't miss what you never really had. As long as I can take the money I put into the 401k when I make my exit, then I win. I'm not going to sit around and wait for the vested money to materialize from an employer if it means missing out on an opportunity to take another step up the ladder and get closer to my goal. Especially if to get the money would mean I would lose a little bit of my career upward progression or lose a little bit of my soul to get it. I don't want to do that. Money you can make back, you cannot recoup a piece of your soul.

At the end of things, on our last day here on earth, we are not going to look back and say, *"I should have stayed with Company X two more years and I could have gotten that vesting money."* I don't think that's going to happen. I think we'll say thank goodness we made the choices we did; that we lived the best life we could live. I think that's what I am about and most interested in. That's what drives me, motivates me, and keeps me career focused.

And perhaps as we discuss it next, you might find this drive to be an equally powerful force in your career progression, and a catalyst for you to own your own succession plan.

CHAPTER FIVE

Carving Out Your Path

The world stands aside to let anyone pass who know where he is going.

— David Jordan

We have to recognize the challenges that exist in business today from a talent perspective—not so much from the generational aspect, but from availability within the marketplace and workforce. More and more, as I watch the news, and read, and talk with colleagues about the fact there are a lot of people out of work. Yet there are companies that still need to get work done.

You would think it makes sense to everyone that if companies have work to get done, they should just hire people and get it done. The challenge is, as many have talked about, organizations don't want to scale back up to the size that they were before the recession hit in 2008. If a 5,000 person organization because of the economy has pared down to 2,500 people; they're not going to ramp back up when the economy turns around. They have had to change their work structure, and the way they do things. They are asking their employees to do more with less. They are asking one employee to do the work of two. Because the economy is so challenged, the employee has no choice. It's either do as you're told or lose your job, and that's not an option for most people.

When executives talk to their employees, and say, "We've really got all this work to get done," and the employees just look at them. It's because the employees are at the breaking point but the company can't hire anybody. So the employees are stuck in the middle and the organization is stuck in the middle. And stuck is not good for the employees or for those organizations. But many consulting firms see the current economic situation as an opportunity for growth.

I think it is a new dawn for the value of the consultant as a thinking partner. Not just, as someone who walks into your organization and tells you what you should do. Instead, the new breed of consultant is someone who can go into an organization and truly partner with them. For me, the definition of partner is more than just showing up and saying, "I am here." A partner is somebody who comes in, sits down, and spends more time looking, listening, and learning, rather than showing up "knowing" all the of answers and begins telling their client what they need to do.

I've seen this happen when some of the major consulting firms (I won't name names) worked with the companies where I was then employed. These large firms come in and the first thing they do is commandeer a conference room and white paper the walls. They start putting up their solution sets based upon what they think are the needs of the organization. That rubs the culture the wrong way. Unfortunately in most large organizations, there are executives (primarily the ones who were advocates for hiring the consulting firm) who watch them come in, go to work, and think, "Wow, these guys are smart so they're going to help us figure out the answers." In reality, they come in with canned answers to client questions—whether they are the right answers or not. The time on site is then spent force fitting current client circumstances into a predetermined solution set, rather than customizing a new solution to a unique set of client issues.

One such firm worked from a document; their standard "Roadmap of Solutions" based on what the needs of the customer would be. It was a great document, very impressive looking. All color-coded and very chic and looked like they spent a lot of money developing this "valuable" knowledge and insight. As an example, this document had a matrix called, "Revenue Generation" and there were rows to address Talent Management, and Compensation & Benefits among other things. It had catchy objectives like, *"Create stakeholder in groups so that stakeholders can feel value in having a hand in crafting the solution."* And they'd tell their client. *"That's what you need to do."* Notice nothing in there discussed HOW the client was to do this for themselves.

It's a good tool to tell you what you need to do, but once the consultants leave; it's up to the organization to figure out the "how." I shook my head in disbelief when I later learned about the company spending millions of dollars to be told what to do, but then left with a shrinking workforce of employees who don't have the necessary knowledge, skill, and ability to how things need to be done. In a lot of instances, the "how" is something that has never been done before, because there are no examples to do what needs to be done. Some Gen Xers don't know how to do it. What ends up happening is that the need for help perpetuates itself. Now that we know what we need to do, we need to go hire another consultant to tell us how to do it. Big consulting firms are known for being masters at stating the obvious. Too many times clients are left bewildered while trying to figure out how to get to the destination pointed to be the firm on their own. I have another anecdotal example from personal experience.

A company with which I am very familiar, hired consultants who came in and spent eighteen months looking at the organization from a structural standpoint, from an HR standpoint, from a talent management standpoint—and discussing what needed to be done. Then they departed, signaling "mission accomplished." The organization would then flounder for about six months, trying to do the "how" of the "what" that they were told. It didn't work. Six months later, they hired a different consulting firm for more millions of dollars to help them decipher what the first consulting firm told them they should do—only now, to help grow this skill set internal to the organization for how to address it. That didn't work so well either, to the point where that consulting firm got booted out of the organization. After all this time and money spent, you were left with a huge pile of documentation about what should be done, and a few documents on how it ought to be done. But you still don't have the people internally who can do it.

What that's led to is the organization saying, "We've got to go find people who can do this. We've got to hire them." So now they are going out and trying to hire Gen Xers to find the 'how' of the 'what' and then actually achieve what these two consulting firms have told them they need to do. But like most companies—they try to find one person to fill the role of change agent. They want to go find the uber-specialist who can do it all. Here's the part that kills me. Because they spent so much money on the consulting, they don't have a lot of money to throw at this person. So if they do find someone, they're going to make them a senior manager or director; a nice job and a nice six-figure salary with a bonus structure. The problem is that person is not an officer of the company. This is a critical flaw in thinking and why that scenario rarely will lead to an actual solution for the organizations.

Who are most of the conversations about talent management, succession planning, and the challenges in organization going to be held with? Officers of the company; the executives who are responsible to ensure there's a bench of top talent for the future. It's been my experience that if you're not an officer of the company, it is very tough to talk to vice president or senior executives about what they need to be doing. It can be intimidating for a non-executive to point out to executives how they should be effectively working their part of the organization to be successful for the future. But organizations tout that one person who is supposed to come into the organization and champion talent management. They're going to help get things tightened up in the organization and put in place and take action on the "how" to satisfy what needs to be done.

After about six months, the newly hired "change agent" realizes they are alone on an island. They realize much too late that the work that they've been brought there to do is bigger than just one person. They're alone because many Baby Boomers in the organization, while they understand that talent management is a need, don't understand the urgency of the need, because it doesn't affect them. And quite frankly, when you start talking about making sure that you have the talent for the future, in a way, it's a backhanded slap to those who are there now, saying, *"Yeah, I know we've got you now, but we need to be planning for when you're not here, or for the skills you don't have and we don't plan to develop you over the time you have left."* How do you do that as a junior level Lone Ranger in a large organization? Not well, or not at all without deep and proper support. That's one of the biggest challenges that organizations have with talent management. Putting a body on it without support is like putting a Band-Aid on broken arm. It shows everyone you made an effort, albeit a visibly poor one that was made without understanding the issue or problem you are trying to solve.

How do you solve for the talent needs of tomorrow while not disrupting the business of the organization today?

That's the dilemma in play that needs to be resolved. Do we have a recruiting and staffing function? Yes, we do. Are they charged with finding talent? Yes. But are they doing it proactively or reactively? Rarely is it proactive. Instead it resembles something quite different ...

"There's an opening we need to fill. John Jones just left the organization."

"Who is John Jones' replacement?"

"Well, it would be Melissa Smith, but she's not ready yet."

"How long will it be before she's ready?"

"She could probably be ready in six to twelve months."

"We can't wait that long; we need to go outside and hire somebody now."

The executives reach out to the internal recruiting and staffing function. Recruiters will have to find someone to fill this person's place. But how do you compensate for this person having a very specific, niche skill set?

Recruiters, by and large, don't have that network of people with niche skills. They don't know where to go find these people, so the recruiter will engage some search firm on a contingency search, or sometimes retained search if it's big enough. "We need this person who can tie his shoes effectively. We don't know where to look for them and they are probably not in our market, and it's probably going to cost us a lot of money to get them here. We don't have the network. Can you help us? Can you be an extension of us to help us get this person so that we can satisfy our internal client?"

So the call goes out and all the search firms smell money in the water, because they know this is a high-priority find and if we can get this person for X Company, they can get 35% of that person's annual salary. If you think about it that sounds like a lot and it is when you do the numbers. If I go out and try to find somebody, and this person's salary is $200,000, if I, the headhunter, place that person, that's $70,000 in my pocket. Nowhere in there did you hear me, the headhunter, say "I want to make sure that this person stays with your organization, I want to make sure that they're the right fit." That's assumed that this comes out in the interview process and the whole courting process, but not necessarily. So I, as the headhunter, place that person, I get $70,000 from you, and I go on my way.

The organization thinks they've won—they got what they needed. The person's there for six to nine months and it doesn't work out. They leave the organization. The loss to the organization is, not only that $70,000, it's also the amount of time that person was ramping up to speed. They say on average it takes six months for a new leader or manager to get up to speed, where they are actually contributing. So half of a $200,000 year or $100,000 is lost (or potentially wasted, in this context), getting the person to the point where they are a value-add as opposed to a straight cost. Now we are up to $170,000 lost. Then you have to look at the impact of not having the right person in the job during a critical time. And that boils over into time to hire. If the person leaves on the first of August, and the company can't find a replacement until the first of January; the time that that seat is empty—a critical, needed role—could be anywhere from $3,500 to $4,000 a day of opportunity cost, lost to the business. It becomes exponentially damaging to hire one person and put them in the wrong setting (because of flawed understanding and assumptions then having that person realize, "Wait a minute, something's wrong with this picture," and they leave the organization.

Allow me to introduce a National Football League (NFL) analogy that's appropriate to the scenario just outlined. First round NFL draft picks are famously often busts. This happens because sometimes they (the agent, the coaches, the employee executives making decisions) force it. They want to believe that that's the guy they need and must have. They overlook some of the little issues that should be part of the decision-making process.

Professional football right now mirrors the corporate hiring environment for a Millennials and Gen Xers. When I say that, Gen Xers ask, "What do you mean?" It's simple. Millennials are pretty much the draft class—as the crop of employees who are coming up those organizations are expecting to come in and be with the team for the foreseeable future. Organizations posture to get and hire the best of the best. The expectation is it's going to take a couple years, but you're going to turn into something great and you're going to carry the organization to a place either it's never been or hasn't been to in a very long time.

Gen Xers however are the free agents. We've been in the league for a while, have seen two or three different teams, have been lots of different places still have sharp skills, and have won and lost and learned from both outcomes. We sign with a team for three years, then that team for the next three years. As Gen Xers, we are the ones signing the short-term contracts, because we're free agents. We'll go wherever they feel we can make an impact, where they can get the most money on a one-year deal (because it's all about the guaranteed money), where we can add to their resume or skill set or pedigree. And it's got to be somewhere where it gives us the type of work-life balance flexibility we want.

When you tell employers that, *"Free agency is basically how Gen Xers think"* that scares the crap out of them. Employers (Baby Boomers) think there should be some loyalty quotient there. If you do work for them, not unlike a free agent signing a contract for multiple years... and then one year into the three years, you want your contract *reworked because you've over performed. You see the owners (organizations) saying, "We're not paying you any more money. You signed a contract. This is what it's going to be."* It's like that in the corporate world between the employer and the Gen Xer. The Gen Xer feels, *"You brought me in here to do this work. I want to do this work. I want to be successful. I want to win. But I am expecting that you're also going to put the best team around me to allow us to win together."* You hear that all the time on ESPN Sports Center, *"He's a great player but he doesn't have the team around him to get to the playoffs ... to win a championship."* Or, *"He carried the team to the playoffs, and when he got there, he ran out of gas."* There are a lot of NFL parallels to what goes on with senior management and executive positions within large organizations with regard to talent management.

Many organizations are floundering or are really rocked by what's happened since 2008 with the economy. Downturns and rough patches happen, it is part of business. Certain industries are cyclical; they have off years at different times because of impact from consumer demand (or lack of) or the commodity, raw material and sometimes even real estate prices that affect their cost structure. The last four years, virtually every business has been affected by what's going on. Large organizations see now that their way of catering to certain high-profile executives and trusting that they're running these companies the right way failed. They were forced to see that the emperor had no clothes. However, there are signs that some sanity may be returning.

Boards of Directors and certainly business owners now think a little bit differently—at least the smart ones are. They are trying to find out, "How do I build a strong, stable organization that I know can perform well year in, year out, no matter what's going on? How do I develop or find employees with talent that gives me that agility, that flexibility to adapt." You can't do it with one person if you put them in scenario I sketched out previously. They can be the next Einstein—or the most experienced person on the planet—but if you don't have the right pieces and support around them, the layer of management that makes the business work; then you will not sustain performance. It's betting everything on one person's abilities. It's not going to work because the pressure to succeed can be paralyzing.

Organizational "lip service" is rampant and will never go away. It's the same in sports, too. A team that year in and year out says, "We want to win now." They put all their eggs in the basket of winning now. (I root for one of those teams.) To switch sports, let's take a look at Major League Baseball (MLB) for a moment. I am a proud 30-year fan of the Boston Red Sox. For the Red Sox, it's always all about winning now. It's great if they happen to get some guys that look like they are going to be around for a while, they'll be a part of the farm team and come up through the ranks and they can count on them later. But that's not the goal. The goal is to win now. Every year, their goal is to win now.

Employees (and organizations) need to understand how counter-productive that is to long-term health. Sports organizations get ridiculed for it. Think about the poor Kansas City Royals. They're always building for next year or some year yet to come. Everybody else that they're playing in the league with is all about winning now. So what happens? The "win now" teams poach the talent out of the Royals and take their talent, because they're not trying to win now.

That's also at play here in the corporate space. There are headhunters making calls today, trying to take somebody from an organization that has been told by the organization, "We're growing you for the future. You're on our farm team. We know who you are. We're going to feed you well, pay you nicely, but you're not going to get a chance to be in a starting role (senior manager or director) any time soon. But you've got a job and we like you a whole lot. So just hang loose."

They're telling that to a Gen Xer or, heaven forbid, a Millennial,

"Just hang loose."

"Really? Why should I?"

"Because you're our future."

"Could you define future?"

"Within the next five to ten years."

Sounds like the organization has issued you a first class ticket to being stuck in the middle.

CHAPTER SIX

Keeping the Talent, Saving the High-Potentials

*Do your work with your whole heart and you will succeed–
there's so little competition.*

– Elbert Hubbard

There is a question organizations need to ask (and answer) so that they don't become stuck in the middle as discussed previously. That question is "How do we keep our top talent engaged and retained?"

There are ways to get Gen Xers to stay with the organization. You can build them up to be your top talent. And if you have top talent inside your organization, you can bind them to the organization, which means you give them restricted stock units, you give them a pay raise or you might give them an in-line promotion. Basically you give them a bunch of love, leeway, lies, and loot to buy their allegiance. You are hoping to buy their time in the seat. You are hoping to buy their career aspirations. You are hoping to buy yourself time.

Companies are starting to also wake up to the fact that, once upon a time, they could say to top talent, "We'll give you a stay bonus of $25,000. If you leave within a year, you've got to pay that money back." But now, that no longer works. Talented individuals with unique, skills in demand can ask for a $50,000 signing bonus somewhere else, take $25,000 to pay back employer number one, and have $25,000 in their pocket courtesy of their new employer . At the end of the day, they get their $25,000 and get themselves unstuck from the middle.

When you say that to organizations that think, "Oh, but we've got a stay bonus for them," they're not going to stay. Because if they're worth you paying that bonus; they're worth twice that to someone else. Another organization that truly recognizes top talent will pay that bonus gladly to get that knowledge, or skill, or ability they don't have currently in their organization.

The Center for Creative Leadership (CCL) talks about the talent development as a 70-20-10 rule. In this rule, 70% of learning and building bench strength for the future is based on a variety of challenging assignments and projects—basically on-the-job experience. 20% is from connecting with others; getting candid feedback, learning by observing, coaching, mentoring, active role modeling. 10% is on coursework and training. The majority of corporate organizations use training, or learning and development, as a way to prepare their leaders for the future—to grow the talent they need. I am by experience a learning and development professional. After I had a cup of the "stand and salute" strength coffee, I realized that training is a reported $90 billion (with a "B") dollar business, yet it is only a 10% solution to what really should be done to drive employee professional development. As such, I now look to training courses as the last or least impactful way to grow knowledge, and skills. I have been forever converted to now be a follower of the 70-20-10 model ... and heavily focused on the 70%, and 20% as evidenced by the crux of this book.

CCL conducted interviews of over 100 top CEOs who told them, "We don't focus on training. Training is not the answer. Training's not meeting the mark. We need employees who can think, who can act." When I think about talent management, for those folks who are stuck in the middle; they're stuck not because they don't have the training to do what needs to be done. It's because they don't have the other two aspects of development being provided for them, or they are not seeking it for themselves the other 90%. They don't have someone who gives them challenging assignments and allows them to observe and learn from others, or who acts as an active role model for them. They don't have someone who coaches and mentors them while providing candidate feedback.

On top of that, the 70% highly visible, challenging assignments that stretch you and help you grow professionally, who are those reserved for in the organization? The high potentials of course. So if you're not deemed "high potential," what do you do? Do you sit around and hope to be rated "high potential" one day? Or do you go and look for an organization that will allow you to be the high potential that you believe you are now but that your company says you may be in five years. I suggest that you go find that company and be their high potential walking in the door today. Be a free agent. Get unstuck by having the role you want now rather than wonder why there is no corporate loyalty at your current employer. Shift your mindset from the job being the most valuable asset in the relationship to instead seeing your time and talents as the most valuable asset.

One of the things mentioned in a recent HR industry magazine is that there are many ways to develop the high potentials; how to hold onto them. I won't go off on too far of a tangent about it, but I think some of the articles I read are funny in a common sense sort of way. Some of the things that they mentioned were suggestions of, "Tell them that they're special" and "Delegate real responsibility." That goes right to that 70%. Some leaders don't want to delegate big, hairy, audacious assignments to their employees, because of their fear that they are going to fail. And it is that their employees' failure will come back to embarrass them.

In reality, that's the thing that we as Gen X leaders want. We want the challenge. We want to go and try to do something significant to see if we can do it. To be kept in the dark and fed "fertilizer" like mushrooms is not what Gen Xers want. The article goes on to suggest: "Be flexible." "Show them that they matter." "Tap effective mentors for them." "Make learning and advancement seem never-ending." "Focus on developing attributes a leader will need." "Give managers assessment tools they need and will use for selection." That is all long-term thinking, which is not being done. Because there's no time … or should I say no time to do these things right. The article I mentioned lays this out nicely. Sometimes just knowing what to do is all that some leaders need in order to make a change.

Organizations are killing themselves trying to figure out how to keep top talent. But in reality, they're failing because they don't understand top talent. They don't understand Gen Xers because they keep shooting in the dark for what they think we want, while at the same time having to run the business of today. They can't give us, Gen Xers, what we want, because it's counter-cultural. I just came from a very large organization where the leader headed a multi-generational group, inclusive of Baby Boomers and Millennials. The leader espoused that we couldn't move to flexible work arrangements or work from home because it would send the wrong message to our internal customers. What message was the leader actually sending? "You can't work remotely because you're not trusted, so if I can't see you at your desk that means to me you're not actually working."

When a Gen Xer walks into an organization and finds out there's a hidden lack of flexibility in work arrangements, they start to think about leaving almost immediately: "I can't grow here. I can't have my career and have my family here. I will be forced to choose." When corporations decide you have to be here to be seen as productive, you have to be here in order to advance, Gen Xers start to figure out how soon can they not be there and I mean in the long term sense. It becomes a conflict over talent management, and a clash that does not always have to occur.

Gen Xers frequently ask me, "How can I have the career that I want to have, the work-life balance and flexibility that I need to have, and the family I love to have?" They're sitting there thinking, "I can't do it; I can't be in corporate America and have the work-life balance I want." I think work-life balance doesn't exist in most organizations because many Baby Boomer leaders are still running their team, division, or department with that 1970s mentality of "you have to be here now."

I just think there's a miss there for our generation to have somebody to speak for them. I have grown weary of hearing from Baby Boomer authors about what is on the mind of Generation X in the workplace. So I decided to add my voice to the conversation as both a Gen Xer, and an author. There's a missed opportunity here for this audience to be able to pick up a book and try to understand what Baby Boomers and Millennials think of us. Does anyone really understand us? Is anyone speaking up for me? Allow me, through the pages of this book, to speak up for Generation X and speak to what you need to know about us as Gen Xers. No matter what you may have been told, what Gen Xers want is in the workplace is really not that complicated.

Show up as a leader with the who, the what, the when, the where, and the why of what you need us to do, and then get out of our way and let us figure out the how to get it done. Give us feedback, both constructive and confirming. Give us that feedback, and allow us to make course corrections instead of holding a grudge against us for not doing it your way. Stop looking over our shoulder every five minutes. Don't freak out because we didn't come into work until 9:00.

These are just a few examples of what we Generation X employees really want, and why organizations need to look at how we get our work done and consider a redefinition of the workplace to be more inclusive of Gen Xer style preferences.

To me as a Gen Xer, my workplace is anywhere that I can get wireless. Anywhere I can get online and have a power outlet, and I will be as productive—more productive—out of the office than in the office. Many Gen Xers are that way too. I can take conference calls or do whatever I need to do especially when every meeting request has conference call information in the body of the invitation. I can be on instant messenger and available to you all day. Why do I have to come into a building simply to log time sitting in an office? I think that's one of the biggest pieces that Gen Xers are struggling with today. There are more appealing, productive things we could be doing instead of just sitting in an office twelve to fourteen hours a day. I had to speak up for my group—in this book—for my frustrated generation who says, "I don't know if I want to do this corporate thing anymore."

What's funny is that most Gen Xers who say they don't want to do that corporate thing anymore are those who have made it to a high enough level to see enough—or maybe they've seen too much of what corporate America is all about. I think about that from my own perspective and the before mentioned discussion I recall having with a senior executive at the last organization that I was a part of, who said, "To move up you have to give up. The higher you go, the more you have to give up." What? That caused a schism for me. I'd always thought, the higher you move up, the more freedom you have, the more autonomy, the more money in your pocket certainly, the more visibility; hopefully more of the financial means to live well, to be with your family more, to go wherever.

No, no, no. I was naïve and misinformed to the reality that the higher you move up, the less time you're actually not at work or tapping away on your Blackberry. The more times you're up early in the morning before your family gets up, banging away on your work issued laptop. The later you stay in the office. The more business trips you go on. The more that's expected of you. The more you're watched. The more you're probed. The more you're quoted. I saw it first-hand that once you get to the executive level, to move up, you get a lot of things that you don't want and give up many of the things that you'd like to keep.

Unfortunately, I think a lot of my Gen X colleagues don't realize that. Some have said, like I said over ten years ago, "I really want to make Vice President." Do you really? Do you really want to have to watch what you say, how you say it, who you're sitting next to, what you wear, where you spend your weekend, how much of yourself you divulge at the office, what you can display in your office. Do you really want to do that? Do you really want to have to sit in meetings and go along with things you don't believe in just because to not do that would be seen as not being a team player? Do you want to have your innovative ideas changed, buffeted, and twisted in such a way that when they come back to you, you don't even recognize them anymore? Do you want to be someone other than yourself? Do you like sitting in the middle seat on a crowded plane for a flight? Do you like being stuck in the middle?

CHAPTER SEVEN

The Big Picture

Only undertake what you can do in an excellent fashion.
There are no prizes for average performance.

– Brian Tracy

The big picture of owning your own succession plan is figuring out what you want, and by figuring that out, figuring out what your plan should be to achieve your desired career success without losing your authentic self.

One thing I want to be clear on; though I state pretty strongly my opinion on what could be done differently with regard to talent management in organizations ... this is not an anti-organization book. It is instead, as subtitled, a Generation X view of miscues in talent management that both employees, and organizations make which stifle individual career passion, and hinder organizational success in the area of talent management.

With the changes the economy has gone through the past couple of years, many organizations now know, for the most part, that they have to change the way that they think. It's not an industrial-age business environment any more. You can't treat employees today like factory workers. You can't hire a superstar as the one person that's going to fix your organization and make it all better. It's about team building. That's a cliché I know, and I hated hearing it used over and over in meetings. But, it really is about building a team-based leadership structure. And everyone's a brick in the wall. Every individual and organization as an entity has their own personality and ego. It is however a collective ego, a collective culture. By understanding both—defining and then examining the best way to make things work better.

I think something that's happened culturally in our society over the last ten or fifteen years or maybe even over the last 20 years. The culprit behind or responsible for many of problems we face as individuals and organizations is society's need and demand for instant satisfaction and instant gratification in all aspects of life—especially career. Sadly, nothing of real value in life comes from simply pushing a button to obtain. So, what we're talking about is as much a philosophy as it is about specifics methods of how you can get unstuck from the middle. There is no button that you can push to simply get unstuck.

Being stuck in the middle is not only something that happens to an individual; there are organizations too that are stuck. They are stuck between that '70s mindset of how to run their business—again, very monolithic even hidebound in some ways—and the needs of the today's multi-generational, virtual working, work-life balance demanding workforce.

As Gen Xers, we no longer want to be tied to a desk in the corporate office for 60 hours a week. We no longer want to put on our corporate uniform (a business suit is still a uniform) and troop off to drab tan cubicle farm or a row of sterile offices just like our Baby Boomer colleagues have every day for decades—almost like lemmings going off of a career cliff. The workforce isn't like that today. It's very different and there are numerous diverse dynamics at play above and beyond just generational difference. Gen Xers specifically have choices of where to work. And those of us considered top talent have still even more choices. Our discussion in this book is about bringing out both an organizational perspective and an individual perspective—the good and the bad as it relates to getting unstuck from the middle from a Gen Xer perspective.

As an individual, you can't constantly live off of the organization feeding you the line, "You have a lot of opportunity here." If the opportunity doesn't show up, you're spinning your wheels. If you're being told, "In five or ten years, you'll get that shot," that's hard to swallow for a Gen Xer that's got any level of ambition. Do you want to spend what could be one quarter of the years you have left here on Earth hoping for career success? Do you want to deny your career passion simply because it may be different than anything you have done professionally to this point?

Assuming you are around 40 years old, ten years could be one quarter of your living years and one half of your viable (remaining) career working years. Organizations need to understand that it is with this perspective that some Gen Xers are thinking and re-thinking their career choices. Organizations need to begin planning for this shift in thinking as they bring practice to their talent management philosophy if they expect retain top talent. "Wait and see" is not a career strategy when the gift of tomorrow is guaranteed to no one.

Any Gen Xer that has worked for any number of years at any level is going to understand the cold truths of what we've touched on so far. Because it's not just an individual business thing; it is a systemic, corporate America cultural thing. At any level or size of bureaucracy you have these issues. They are common. They have to be addressed. They have to be changed, because, again, organizations get stuck too. The ones that remain stuck will never reach their potential of being an employer of choice. They will flounder. Worse yet, if you're not moving ahead as a company or an organization and this is true even as an individual, then you run the very real risk of every progress that you have made slipping away from you. I remember my high school football coach saying, "Either you are getting better or you're getting worse. You're not staying the same." It's the law of the universe. It's just the way it is. Staying the same is staying stuck in the middle.

CHAPTER EIGHT

An Integrated Talent Solution

Analyzing what you haven't got as well as what you have is a necessary ingredient of a career.

— Orison Swett Marden

For all the issues and challenges I've mentioned that face organizations in the area of talent management; there is an integrated, talent solution that when customized for their culture, will present solutions for them.

How do I buy, borrow, or build the talent I need for tomorrow while running the business that I need to run today? What is the right mix of things for your organization in the 70-20-10 model we discussed earlier—that will arrive at developing the management and leadership bench strength the company needs long-term? Does it really need to be 70-20-10? The answer can be found by devoting the time and focus to look, listen, and learn the needs of the organization. You have to ascertain who the organization is today and who they want to be tomorrow, and help address and close the gap between what you find. That gap is another instance of where organizations and individuals are stuck—in the middle between whom they are and who they want to be.

There's rarely a natural bridge across the valley between who you are and who you want to be. The only way to get there from here is to go down to and cross the valley floor, and come back up the other side. You can either do that the hard way or the easy way. There is a path, but individuals and organizations can't or don't always see it easily. I believe, because I've spent time crossing many career valley floors for myself, that I can see the path for others. So what I want to do is be a career Sherpa get Gen Xers to go from one side of the valley to the other, to get you where you want to be. To help you to realize the fact that, you've spent a lot of time on your own in learning and development land, in what I now call "10% land" only to learn that this alone will not help move you forward. It is not necessarily arriving at the destination, but it is the journey that actually teaches you the most. In business, I think that's as applicable to an individual, as it is to a corporation.

Part of the process I, as a Gen X Sherpa, would employ in guiding individuals and organizations is simple. I would not figuratively just tie a line around you and drag you to where you want to go. Instead I will walk with you, guide you, and say, "Step here. Grab here. Lift here. We're going to pull together here." Before setting out, we would have a detailed plan for the journey all worked out with step-by-step risk mitigation strategies. There is a great deal of teamwork that is involved so that you are not, at any time, left on your own. That becomes part of not only getting you to the destination but also your development and maturation as either an organization or an individual along the way.

Improvement of an organization or an individual comes with a change of thinking based on new information. It has nothing to do with age. It's more about how seasoned is your thinking and have you gathered enough experience or raw career material through application, mentoring, and coaching to use good judgment at the right time. That to me is wisdom, if you boil it down into a single definition. Wisdom comes from not only knowing how to do something, but also when to do it—learned from actual experience. It's gained through what you learn on the journey that enables you not only to get to the immediate destination but also to be prepared to move on further to a new destination not yet planned.

Back to something I talked about earlier. Organizations hire consultants because they think they're going to give them answers. But instead, most are going to state what the problem is and what you need to do. What you need to do is not really the answer. Most often, that's something you will realize anyway.

All solutions for an organization and for individuals really rest within themselves. If you know what the problem is, and you know what you need to do but struggle with either motivation or inspiration to do it, then it's just a matter of having someone external to the issue who has the organization's interests or individual's best interests at heart to be that Sherpa. To be that person who can move you along, who can help you navigate the raging seas of uncertainty and opportunity. Allow me to share a real world case in point example with you.

I was recently contacted by an organization (through a colleague) that needed some help. They wanted a complete human capital strategy and a strategic workforce plan of who they needed to hire and when, but they wanted it through a diversity lens. They are trying to increase their diversity to become a more multi-cultural, and inclusive organization. They are looking to bring in talent that would find a welcoming, diverse environment whether that diversity is of veteran status, color, gender, sexual preference—but do it from a strategic perspective. So we sat down and took a look at the organization, as it was that day, and where they wanted to be tomorrow. We looked at the business strategy and different facets that, when pieced together, provided a picture of the organization of who they were, what talent they needed, when they needed to get them, how they needed to get them, why they needed to look in these places.

And my firm will do something for them that the big boys (major consulting firms) don't do instinctively. They won't look at the organization through a diversity lens. My firm will do all the typical management consultant functions but (and this is a big difference) we'll go and help them find that talent. My consulting firm takes pride in being a true partner in getting clients to where they want to go. We sit with you. We work with you. We're in those crucial meetings with you. We're part of the conversation. We're also a stakeholder. We're part of all the important initiatives. We get to a place where you say, "Okay, now we know where we need to hire. We need to hire seven employees in these critical, special areas. We have a diverse slate of candidates. We're not saying we definitely have to have a person of color, but we definitely want the employees that we look at to be a representative segment of the current society, so that we can say, "let's look at the best qualified candidates who happen to be diverse." Don't just go get diverse candidates. Get the most qualified, and hopefully in that activity, if you really look far and wide, you will by default assemble a diverse slate of candidates.

An integrated talent solution helps to fill the gap between the individual and organization. Within that integrated solution you can either buy the talent that you need for tomorrow, you can borrow it (which I refer to as contract labor), or you can build it by using the 70-20-10 model. Building it means I have to know what I need first. If you know that you need to replace your Chief Underwriter in three years, and you know the person who you've got in my organization who could be ready to take that job will not be ready for three years—what are you doing with that information? Are you going to lavish that person with gifts to make them want to stay? No, you could do that for a while, but five years is a long time. Or do you put a plan in place, based upon contingency, saying, "If this person leaves before the three years it will take to get someone internal ready, I can either hire (buy) somebody which most companies do, I can use contract labor (borrow) to fill that spot for the short term; but for a senior role that has to do with the internal workings or trade secrets, that's not going to be an option." So the need to build and build early comes back into play. Give the role to an identified person early and fast track their readiness to see what happens. However, you can't do that if you don't know what talent resources you have in your company. But you must have a plan for them once you realize you have them as a possible solution to the looming loss of your current underwriter.

Buying or hiring externally to fix every talent gap sends the wrong message.

This is the reactionary move that I mentioned earlier. From the HR perspective, we lost an employee. We've got an opening; now we've got to fill it now. That's not proactive. And it's not that you are planning for Alex to decide to leave because someone poached her. It's that you have a plan to build the talent around her, within her direct reports, so that you can slot in the next right person at the right time. They've earned that. If the opportunity is there, then you have talent identified who will be best prepared for this opportunity if and when it comes along.

I know this from my own perspective, and I would imagine that you do too. Someone comes to you and says, "Alex is leaving. We think you're the person for that job." Immediately you feel appreciated. You feel wanted. That's an important part of working for an organization—to feel appreciated. Hopefully, the appreciation turns into real, long-term appreciation. In other words, not simply we love you now just because we need you, or because you fit into our crisis picture. But it's actually quid pro quo. It turns into that opportunity and not they're just trying to stick their finger in the dyke because there's about five thousand gallons of water on the other side that's going to pour in because of Alex's departure. You don't want to be anyone's stopgap. You want to believe that you are now and always were the long-term solution for them, and that the organization genuinely feels that way about you.

We all hope that the case would be the company actually coming to you and saying, "Alex is leaving and we think you're the person for the job." But the second part of the conversation in an organization that actually practices talent management is, "We think you're the person for the job, but you're about six months away from being ready, so what we'd like to do is give you the shot, but you're going to get heavy mentoring and coaching to ensure you succeed." It becomes a much more positive message of support. Smart leaders in proactive talent management companies realize that this interaction is being watched across the organization for evidence of "walking the talk."

One thing I believe organizations need to be reminded of, told, or shown is that how you treat each employee speaks volumes to the rest of the organization about your value of the current workforce. If you always go out and buy (hire) one talented person after another, you cannot keep preaching the values of talent management, internal growth and development. Your employees are going to question, why you aren't giving employees inside the company a chance. When you repeatedly go outside the company, you are saying one thing and doing another. You add to the hypocrisy that is sadly rampant in today's corporate environment Again reactivity is to blame here along with the absence of proactive talent management in the form of strategic workforce planning.

Every once in a while, a corporation has to wince a little bit, rip off the Band-Aid, and give somebody inside the company a chance. Even if they may not believe the person is a 100% ready for it. This still builds goodwill for the organization. Other employees will comment, "Wow, who got put in that job?" "Mary Smith got it." "It is great news to hear that Mary will be in that role. She's been here a while and she is very sharp. I don't know if she's really ready, but sounds like they're going to do right by her and give her the shot. At least for once they didn't just hire someone from outside the company." That's what employees want to see and hear. They want an organization to do right by them. And the organization, really wants the same from their employees. They want their employees to stay with them and grow. It's a two-way street. But we need to make sure there are parking spots available on both sides of the street.

The thing is, and I'm sure you can probably come up with some exceptions to this, but in general, I don't believe that organizations set out to be malevolent toward their employees. But they often do things that hamper the career potential of individuals that work for them. It doesn't need to be that way.

Better planning and execution can prevent damaging things from happening or certainly mitigate their impact. Building in a set of proactive business processes and developing an employee-centric philosophy can reduce the scale of damage when it comes time to making tough business decisions involving job reductions or layoffs of your talent.

So as individuals have to figure who they are and who they want to be, organizations also need to figure out exactly who they are and who they want to be in the future. The result is that both go into that employee-employer transaction with a clearer understanding of the path for the organization and the individuals. But to really work out what's the right angle, you have to understand the other's position, because you can't design your career path without knowing where you want that path to lead.

For companies to improve and completely immerse themselves in twenty-first century employee and talent management practices, there has to be a change in their way of thinking of what they need to do for their employees.

This book is also positioned as a tool, a look into the Gen Xer sentiment to help companies figure out many of these challenges. It is these thoughts shared here that with a change in mindset, can help companies realize that their employees do want to work for them, but that they expect more than they're getting. I believe there is a way that the objectives of both the individual and the organization can be met. It just takes approaching it the right way and then executing a strategy to make it happen so that the two sides neither get, nor stay stuck in the middle.

CHAPTER NINE

Learning is Like Breathing

Learn how to be happy with what you have while you pursue all that you want.

– Jim Rohn

Like people, organizations learn. The only problem with organizations is that it is harder for them to make noticeable change as a result of that learning as quickly as an individual. It takes a long time to turn a battleship. Because many organizations think their business is too complex to change. Or, because "things have always been done this way, so we can't do it any different way." At some point reality, the economy, or unforeseen circumstances are going to provide them a rude awakening in the form of losing market share or facing quarterly losses in the millions. This happens primarily because one year ago, five years ago, ten years ago, they didn't do the things they should have done to prevent ending up where they are right now. And some of what was not done involves securing top talent—not finding or keeping key people critical to the health of the company.

Like humans, businesses can also die from a thousand cuts. They can bleed out. Most consultants are good at pointing out any problems or issues but provide very little on how to deal with them. You have to analyze the current state and what got you to this place, you are then able to identify the root cause of the problem. You have to address that root cause to get at your solution and then make changes where they are absolutely necessary. And just as a problem is often built on a series of small things gone or done wrong ... the solution itself may be one of many iterations or sub tasks. You take care of this first, then you take care of this second, and then you take care of the third. Ultimately, you may end up with a total solution to that particular issue. But do you have the patience to solve issues, in that way, and over time?

As individuals, it is important to understand it's acceptable to not know everything. I don't know everything. I know a lot about one thing. And that one thing is talent management from a common sense perspective. That's it. I'm an inch wide and a mile deep on talent management and the associated change management processes that allow and facilitate the use of an integrated strategy to deploy talent management strategically and effectively in organizations As mentioned before, it is important that before you start down any path as an organization (for that matter as an individual too) you need to figure out who you are and who you want to be, and know the desired destination you want to reach. Not where others tell you where you need to be, not who other tell you that you need to be. The desired destination should be that place where you can be who you WANT to be.

That's the answer that everyone thinks that they're getting when they are mentored by someone like they "need to be" in corporate America. Everyone buys what they think is the "success solution" but they fail to manifest any change in themselves or the organization—because they never really understood where they wanted to go from the very beginning. They instead are buying transportation to a destination others believe they need to get to—and when they get there they realize, "Wait a minute... this isn't what I wanted!" Of course not! You allowed yourself to look at your career through the eyes of someone else instead of your own. You looked at your career reflection in the mirror of someone else who see things differently than you do. You didn't listen to yourself... the one person who matters the most. I've experienced this myself recently. I chased after what I believed, and what society had helped me to believe was what I needed, who I needed to be, where I needed to be. Only when I got there did I realize that this was not for me. In that moment I asked myself how did I get here, and where exactly in my career am I?

This happens to organizations too. And it's even harder for an entire company to make changes, there's more inertia, more ego, higher visibility and more resistance. It's the combination of mass and momentum. If a company founder or owner never really asks the question of the senior leaders, "In five years, are we going to be the organization that we want to be or where Wall Street believes we should be?" Then, it's just every day the same-old same-old, it's rolling along, rolling, and rolling but not thinking, "Are we really moving this thing towards where we want to be?"

The questions to ask and answer (one at a time) are: "Do we want to be better in five years so that we're leaner, more profitable?" "Are we doing the right things for our employees?" "Are we running the risk of them having the carpet pulled out from under us, because they have a job that we didn't really want them to have?" "And if that happens, what does that say for the health of the company?"

Managing expectations is important. This is especially true with corporations. They often have a vision of where they think they need to go—of who they are and how Gen Xers see them—but often they don't really understand what they want to be as an organization. Organizations sell jobs to employees that think, "This is where I need to be." But when things go wrong and they wake up from the sleep of missed opportunity there are always many excuses, "It's because we didn't think. We didn't know the economy was going to do this".

The fact is if you build with a purpose, you know and understand your intent and what makes a strong, solid organization—the types of organizations that survive economic instability—you can then be a strong, solid organization. There are companies that have made money steadily for 30, 40 years, 50 years. How? They built a plan to survive any twist and turn. An example I would suggest is Southwest Airlines. How do they turn a profit every year of their existence in one of the most screwed up, competitive industries ever? Simple ... they have the best people for their specific business. Notice I did not say the best people in THE business. They focused on extreme differentiation from their competitors through their people. That's what you have to do as an organization: figure out what are some of those fundamental things that companies who are successful in talent management have had long-term success doing with their top talent.

I was talking recently with someone who is totally disenfranchised with the organization he works for. He believes he's been passed over for promotion two times. He's stuck it out and he's tried, but he's at the five-year mark and feels, "I am done with this. I'm not getting what I want out of this. They're not seeing me as being anything more than whom I was when I walked through the door five years ago." He is leaving that organization as soon as he can. He has decided that waiting and hoping of a promotion or to be seen as high potential had run its course with the organization.

What's interesting is that there are more and more Gen Xers waking up from their slumber of suffering silence and saying, "I'm not having fun. I'm not getting what I wanted out of this.

This is just not where I want to be." Organizations do not hire you based on who they believe you can become with them. Instead, they sell you on your fit with the organization for who you currently are. They hire you for what they need you to be, not who you want to be. They don't care who you want to be ... you can be who you want to be after hours. And what happens is that perception can be shifted so that it really becomes more of blaming yourself saying, "Okay, I just am not cut out for this." First you blame yourself. Then you blame the organization. Finally, when you run out of things, people, or circumstances to blame, what are you left with? You're left with the very thing you started with: the situation at hand, and how you react and respond to it. Are you going to look deep enough, whether organizationally or individually, to find out that these are my own succession planning character flaws, these are my organizational talent management flaws, and these are my other shortcomings? These are the things that I know I am not good at or that I know that I can't do or we can't do, so we need to focus on the things that we can do. This is our path to being a stronger organization or a successful individual. When you do this, the path across the valley floor we discussed earlier comes into clear view from almost any vantage point.

CHAPTER TEN

You don't have to be who they think you need to be

I won't miss you. I will miss who I thought you were.
- Anonymous

There is certainly a hypocrisy that both organizations and individuals end up assuming—and acting out. We all think we need to present ourselves as someone that is maybe not necessarily us, but who is someone the organization needs us to be. And it is this tug of war that keeps Gen Xers stuck in the middle again between who they need to be as opposed to who they really want to be, or as opposed to being their authentic self.

Any time that you make your decisions based on what you think someone else is going to think, you're headed down the wrong path in life. No matter the trappings of success you acquire, or the money you make, when you aren't being who you really are you're never going to really be happy. It's a negative compromise. It's negative because you compromise who you are, or your family, or your health, or your sanity for a big salary, a lofty title, a corner office, a big house, or an expensive car. All of these trappings are nice and society will tell you that by having them you have done well. But if to get these things and keep them you have to become someone else, do you really ever have them? Or are they really the possessions of someone else who just looks like you? Are they a burden on your life and career because to keep them means playing a character role day in and day out?

Hypocrisy in organizations creates or exacerbates the "lack of being your authentic self" issues and problems many Gen Xers face daily. One such hypocrisy is companies who say publicly, on their websites, in their core values, and in their mission statements that "our people are our greatest asset/resource." Yet they do not have a true talent management strategy or philosophy, where they actually groom and grow employees within the company. These companies do not prepare ahead of time so that when they lose employees, they are able to have proactive rather than reactive course of action to finding top talent to replace the employees who depart. It's about building the bench strength long before the employees on the bench ever need to get in the game. It's about building the organization. And that's the thing that best serves individuals too, so that they don't feel stuck, so they don't feel like "I can't work here anymore." Or feel like "The minute another company makes me an offer; I'm so gone from this dead end place."

These thoughts, and the personal conversation with self for most of us as Gen Xers will always be part of life as a professional. That is of course until you find you career passion. Until you can show up to work every day as your real self. If the organization learns how to do the right things for the individuals, it runs a better chance at slowing down turnover. The organization runs a better chance of building more bench strength, because you are developing employees, and those individuals are satisfied with what's going on within the organization. They feel like they are part of something, and they're not then as susceptible to wanting to jump ship.

Getting unstuck from the middle starts with knowing that you're stuck—understanding it and admitting, "I'm stuck and I've got to get out." That's the truth of it. Looking at and understanding how you got there. Becoming unstuck, whether it's as an organization or as an individual all starts with an honest assessment. Be honest with yourself "Am I where I want to be?" It's the same thing for organizations. Be honest about what's going on in your organization. Call it like it is. That's why sometimes you need to have someone external point those things out to you. It is the reason why I wrote this book to give a name, a face, and definition to what many feel every day, but do not know what to call it. By viewing your situation honestly, even though the true state may not be what anyone wants to hear, you can define the problem. And once defined, you can figure out the real actions to take to address the problem and make it go away. And better yet, now that it is defined, you can use the warning signs to allow you to proactively prevent it from happening again.

If organizations can employ some of the tools as discussed so far; if employees can act on some of the guidance offered in this book; I believe we can arrive at a place where both organizations and employees will recognize their authentic self, find their passion, and get unstuck so that talent management becomes not just something organizations do, but how organizations and employees co-exist in a healthy environment for both.

CHAPTER ELEVEN

The "Never Out" Job & Understanding Critical Roles

Individual commitment to a group effort - that is what makes a team work, a company work, a society work, a civilization work.

— Vincent Lombardi

Every organization has critical roles that if the right people weren't in them, the organization couldn't function, couldn't deliver on its mission—and at worst, might not remain a viable enterprise long-term without the right people performing in them.

A critical role is defined easily as the "never out" job. The type of job that can never be open, can never go unfilled, and should never be talent misaligned. Take an industry like FedEx. What would you say is the "never out" job at FedEx that allows them to deliver (no pun intended) on their promise to their customer? I would suggest to you it is their drivers. If they don't have drivers, they can't deliver your packages. Without drivers, FedEx could not execute and effectively run their business.

If you look at a hospital, there are many people who work at a hospital. But looking closer at personnel positions, which "never out" job or role, if not filled would prevent the hospital delivering on its number one mission. Which job is the most important in providing care for the sick and wounded? You might think doctors. I'd submit it's the nurses. Nurses protect patients from the risks and consequences of illness, disability, and infirmity, as well as from the risks and consequences of the treatment of illness. Even the most emotional work nurses do is a form of rescue. When nurses construct a relationship with patients or their families, they are rescuing patients from social isolation, terror, or the stigma of illness or helping family members cope with their loved ones' sickness or injury.

Think now of a major (life, health, home, or auto) insurance company. Who are those people with the "never out" job in an insurance company? Who, without them, the company wouldn't be able to insure its customers? I would point to the underwriters. They decide whether insurance is provided and, if so, under what terms. They identify and calculate the risk of loss from policyholders, establish who receives a policy, determine the appropriate premium, and write policies that cover this risk. An insurance company may lose business to competitors if risk underwriting is too conservative, or it may have to pay excessive claims if the underwriting actions are too liberal.

For a final example, let's look at a bank. What is our "never out" job here? I would say that it's the loan officers. Loan officers gather information to determine the likelihood that individuals and businesses will repay the loan. Loan officers may also provide guidance to prospective borrowers who have problems qualifying for traditional loans. For example, loan officers might determine the most appropriate type of loan for a particular customer and explain specific requirements and restrictions associated with the loan. The idea of banking is to bring your money in and give you a small bit of interest for the privilege of holding onto your money, so they can turn around and loan it out to someone else with a higher rate of interest to cover their expenses. Loan officers make the money for the bank, because they grant or deny loans, protecting and ensuring that the bank makes money.

As shown through these examples, every organization has a group of critically skilled individuals who if they do not have a plan for their replacement or the sustainment, or if employees in those were to leave, it would become a major, business-threatening, problem. That's one of the biggest challenges companies face ... how to keep their "never out" jobs from being in jeopardy of being unfilled. However, many companies have not thought of identifying their "never out" jobs and they don't know who the people are who are in those roles today. So logic follows that they cannot then have a proactive approach to replacing one of this critical people to their organization from their internal bench of top talent. But there is a way to solve this shortcoming.

To address those challenges, a talent management focused organization would first define critical roles within the company. And that does not mean a top down look. Many organizations believe that the "never out" or critical role for them is their CEO, COO, CFO, or CIO. If you take those particular leaders out of the organization, many would agree that the organization still would run efficiently and effectively. It might not have the executive leadership at the top that Wall Street would want to see or that the Board of Directors feels like it needs there, but the bottom line is the organization can continue with day-to-day business without much of a hiccup. This disqualifies these roles as being "never out". To illustrate this point, let me paint for a moment with a broad brush by using a military comparison about officers and enlisted personnel onboard a US Navy ship. I must warn you now; I spent 10 years as an enlisted sailor in the Navy. So my opinion here is meant to be satirical (somewhat) and might be slightly biased from an enlisted sailor's perspective.

The parallel to business that I see is you can take all of the officers off of a ship and still expect that ship to do what needs to be done. The ship will get underway, she'll sail, she'll fight, and she'll bring herself back, because the leadership runs through the organization from bow to stern—through the most senior non-commissioned officers (NCOs) all the way down to junior enlisted. But finer points of naval strategy outside of current mission objectives will probably not be as important as the day to day running of the ship. In fact, they may be ignored all together.

On the flip side, if you take all the enlisted off and leave only officers. The ship would rust to the side of the pier as they work to take tactical hands-on action from the strategic viewpoint of bridge. The officers who have a high-level knowledge of strategy, big-picture mission objectives, would struggle if left alone to operate and fight the ship. They may not have the "down to the rudder and screw" knowledge, skill, and ability to get underway.

This is a clear case in point that an organization or a ship has to have both strong strategic and tactical capabilities. And more importantly, you need top talent in these roles to make an impact. Sure, you've got to have great tactical people in place to get things done. But you also have to rely on strategy that has been set by visionary senior leaders, but you don't need the senior leaders in all instances to effectively execute on the business.

I think organizations spend too much time trying to replace the senior leaders and worry too little about the employees who actually get the work done every day. The importance of the people who comprise the middle layer of an organization are the holders of those critical roles, holders of those never out jobs. I term the employees in this middle layer as either Steady Eddy or Steady Betty. The Steady Eddy/Betty group is proud of their work and happy to have their job. They like their career to date. They come to work every day. They've given some quality years to the organization. They expect to see themselves retiring from the organization. But they also want to be developed. They want new opportunities. They want new challenges. They might not necessarily want to move up to be the next senior director or VP, but they like having challenging work. They like to feel like the work that they do matters.

The reason why organizations are losing employees in that talented middle is because they spend too much time focusing on high-potential employees. They are focusing on high potential employees instead of caring for and feeding those folks in the middle who allow the organization to function. I am talking about those senior managers and directors who actually get the work done for you. They're the ones who actually lead the organization. They're the ones who are on the cusp of having the right mix of tactical and strategic to get things done. They are the ones who are on the front line. They have a clear line of sight from the shop floor to the corner offices of senior management.

But some of these employees who do want to grow or progress to levels senior leadership are frustrated because every time there's a senior leader opening in the organization—this is all in generalities—they are forced to watch the organization consistently hire someone outside the company for those roles. They're not being given the opportunity to move into those roles of senior leadership. They're not getting tapped to move into an opportunity where they can grow their skill set to be ready to be the next senior director or Vice President. They're being overlooked. They're suffering from something that I've heard many times in my career and once suffered from personally while being stuck in the middle for a time myself. Many Gen Xers have worked so hard to get where we are today, that we now stuck in the middle from a different perspective.

If you can't be replaced, then you can't be promoted.

That's something a lot of organizations struggle with. They have very skilled, smart, senior people but they are perpetuating this conundrum because they're looking at one of their employees and saying, *"Jill Jones is fantastic. She is the best underwriter we could have ever hoped for. Let's just hope she never leaves. Let's hope that she is doing now all that she would ever want to do."* No one's asking Jill what she would like to do,

"Jill, what do you really want to do?"

"Well, I really want to move over to marketing."

No one's trying to help Jill move over to marketing, because that would mean that Jill wouldn't be our number one underwriter. Leaders in companies can be myopic and selfish because they want to make sure they have key people in key roles so that they never have to worry. As we discussed, we want to make sure that we keep the "never out" jobs filled. But we want to have those roles filled by employees who are both qualified to be there, and also WANT to be there.

What drives the replacement dilemma? From an organizational perspective, there are two components: fear and ignorance. Ignorance will keep Jill in her place by assuming she is where she wants to be because we have not asked her. Fear is at play here too because we're scared what will happen if Jill is not in her role. The desire here is not to nefariously stunt the growth of Jill's career or to flatten her trajectory. It's actually backhanded flattery. Jill has a "never out" job and she doesn't know it. Jill is so great that we can't even imagine ourselves without her being in that role.

Jill was just burned by the drama of if you can't be replaced, you can't be promoted. But what if Jill is burnt out from years of doing the same job she has been doing. What if Jill gets frustrated about not getting the opportunity to do more of what she wants to do in her career? What if Jill becomes resentful of the fact that nobody has even asked her what she wants to do while she watches the company hire someone from the outside into the role she wants and is ready for now. While she may be physically in the role, mentally she may check out if she is not allowed to explore her wants over the organization's needs. She may even get so angry that she leaves the organization for another opportunity with another employer that allows her to be her authentic self AND to have the role she wanted with her previous company.

I've had someone in my career say to me, *"Why would you want to be anything more than a leadership program facilitator? You're so good at what you do. Why can't you just be happy with that?"* To that individual, I replied, *"You don't know me very well. The minute I master something is the minute I need to go find something else to master."* A lot of employees are at mastery in areas that are important to the organization, but they are looking to do something new or different. Sadly many organizations have yet to realize it, and most have yet to allow themselves to think other than one dimensionally about their employees.

How do we know the top talent in our organization? How do we know who the most effective middle managers are in our organization? Once we know that talent, how do we grow that talent to what we need for today, tomorrow, and the future? Once we know who these talented people are, we'll be able to show their talents off to others in the organization. We'll know their strengths. We'll know their points of mastery. We'll know that Jill is a great underwriter but also know that she wants to explore other career options, and that's going to involve some growing. We'll know that Jill would really like to move into a marketing role in six months. We'll know that we should look for an opportunity to flow her into that role. Knowing your talent allows you to purposefully grow, show, and then flow your talent through the organization.

The next two realities I'm going to talk about completely escape many organizations. There are organizations today that are getting it right, and through some of the observations presented in this book, many more in the future will also get it right by facing these realities and employing tactics to support them.

The first reality is that once you know who the talent is in your organization, you can grow it into what you need it to be for today and tomorrow, which allows you to show that talent to others. You can't horde and hide your talented people as part of your organization. You need to show them off. If you're a senior leader and you've got this really talented person like Jill, give her the opportunity to work on a cross-functional marketing project. Give Jill the opportunity to attend the quarterly marketing meeting or to dial into the weekly or biweekly on marketing conference call. By showing off her talent to the leaders in marketing, you will keep Jill engaged, you will keep her growing. By showing her talents off, she continues to build positive notoriety, greater credibility, and influences her brand within the organization. These things are easy enough to do. If you think about it, doing these things together can become a powerful retention tool. It's a powerful tool for employee engagement, for retention, for really building an esprit de corps within an organization. And it's something that's really cost effective. It doesn't cost a lot of money to do any of the things I've just talked about.

Knowing, growing, and showing and then eventually flowing talent through your organization is a way to reward the employees in a non-monetary way, because everyone wants to be appreciated and acknowledged. It is also the top four attributes of an organization with a truly integrated talent management strategy. The barrier of not having funding to support this effort goes out the window because there is no money involved. There's a tremendous upside for an organization to do that. Everyone as a human being acknowledges that it feels pretty good if you get recognized and appreciated. That is as large a component that drives many people as anything else. That's one of those little things organizations can do—leaders giving expressions of appreciation are the right thing to do, and it has that collateral benefit of helping with retention but also the outside perspective of how Gen Xers view your organization from afar. That's something most companies don't think about much from an organizational perspective.

Gen Xers want to have an opportunity to participate and be part of something greater than themselves. Organizations and companies spend a lot of time on mission and values. At the end of the day, for you as employee—whether you are the janitor or the CEO—do you like coming to work? Do you feel like you can be yourself in this organization? Do you feel like you have a career? Do you feel that you have advancement opportunities? Put aside for a moment the mission and the vision. Yes, they're important and you've got to have them, but at the end of the day, do employees feel like this is the right place for them to be? That's got nothing to do with a company's mission, vision, values, or core competencies. It's got to do with the happiness and engagement of the employees. No one's going to go work for (or stay with) an organization just because their mission statement sounds good.

The vision statement is who we want to be now and in the future. The mission statement is how we are going to get there. Values to me are the externally displayed morals of the company. Lastly, the core competencies are the internally used "table stakes" to measure how you act or behave in the company. In my opinion, you need only have one core value and one core competency and it can, in my opinion, be one and the same.

Do the right thing always!

Doing the right thing always at work means do what you're asked to do. Doing the right thing always at work means don't talk about somebody behind their back. Doing the right thing always at work means don't steal. Doing the right thing at work always means show up on time. Doing the right thing at work always means don't add those things to the expense report that you know you didn't really pay for when you travel. Doing the right thing at work always as a leader is to know, grow, show, and flow talent in the organization. That's the quintessential core competency to which everything else you do should connect.

The second reality from the company perspective of doing the right thing always is (1) knowing who the talent is in your organization, (2) growing it in the way of knowledge, skills, and abilities, (3) enabling and supporting talented employees in showing those talents within the organization, and (4) finally

STUCK IN THE MIDDLE

flowing top talent to positions in the organization that are both a match for their career aspirations and the growth of the organization. Do this and Gen Xers in your company will start to feel like they have an identity and you as an organization will be seen as a builder of talented employees and an employer of choice internally. And it is this internal sentiment that will become your external brand. The irony is that the fourth step provides the greatest return, and is the hardest to do.

As an example, I've got this talented person who works for me who I can't really do without. Let's say it is Jill from earlier in our story who wants to be move over to marketing. Then I as Jill's leader, if I am truly committed to the know, grow, show and flow model, would go and sit with my peers in marketing and say,

"I want to work something out with you so that over the next six months, Jill has an opportunity to either shadow one of your folks, or be mentored by you or your folks. She eventually wants to move over to marketing. She is one of my best employees and I support her career progression and want to help her get there."

I would have that conversation in full view of Jill. I would have that conversation in full view of Jill's peers. I would have that conversation in full view of my peers and of my boss. Finally, I would have this conversation if I actually mean to "walk the talk" of our core competency of doing the right thing always.

The question is why are organizations losing Gen Xers at that senior manager, and director level? The answer is because there is a career progression bottleneck. I recently worked for an organization where the average age of the employee was forty-four-years old. Baby boomers may find it startling to think that half of the leadership of this major organization were forty-four years or younger. Even the senior leaders in this organization are young by most standards. Vice presidents were anywhere from late thirties to early fifties. Senior vice presidents were early fifties to mid-sixties. In short, this organization structure is representative of the generational diversity trends in companies of the future.

There was a certain number of vice president slots at this organization and less than one-third of that number at most could ever be available as senior vice president slots, which means if you are promoted to, or come into the organization as a vice president, you're going to be a vice president for a long time before you can make senior vice president. And if you are working for one of these vice presidents as a senior director, it's going to be a long time before you can make vice president. Sure, you can get an in-line promotion. You would get a new title without any more responsibilities—in effect you just get to say you are a vice president and to order new business cards.

Let us get back to our conversation about Jill for a moment. By flowing Jill's talent through the organization this way, what it says is that if I am going to flow Jill to this other opportunity it's going to create a slot, an opening, leaving a "never out" job unfilled. If I know by working with my peer over in marketing, it'll take Jill about six months before she could really move over there, then I'm going to sit with Jill and say,

"If I'm going to work with you to get you ready for this new position, I need to know who you recommend as the person that we should be working with, who is six months away from being able to do your job. Who could step into your role in six months if you move to marketing?"

I would imagine Jill would be highly engaged by both the opportunity to effect change on her career, as well as contribute to building bench strength in the organization. I am not saying Jill should just handpick her successor, but I do think there should be a conversation with Jill about the pros and cons, strengths and opportunities of the people she points out that could fill her role as a holder of a "never out" job.

Playing this example forward, how does this become a real strategy? An idea that has worked is to drive this change through the leaders in the organization, where each leader is required once a year, to flow or move at least one of the highly talented members of their team to another part of the organization—a real top performer. Make that a mandatory requirement. Make it where leaders have to do that as demonstration of their commitment to talent management. Have them be measured on it. Have a substantial percentage of their annual bonus be based on it. Have them and the organization put their money where their mouth is with regard to talent management.

But in many companies this will not happen because there's a strong element of protectionism to maintain the status quo. *"I've got a top performer. I don't want him going anywhere. I'm scared of what's going to happen if he leaves, because I will have to fill a massive void. He makes me look good. I don't want him going anywhere else"*. That's a common mentality of management within an organization. The thing to do is to throw that out, and instead make this behavior part of your corporate culture so that every manager or director or vice president is incentivized to flow people up and through the organization. Not to build silos, but instead to steadily stream talent through the organization.

To use how a tree gets nutrients as an analogy, everything comes up through the root system, and it's manifested in the leaves. Growth doesn't happen if the nutrients are not available to the root system. When nothing can come up through soil and the ground to the trunk, branches, and the leaves... of course, the tree dies.

I believe leaders of the organization, officers, officials, are supposed to do the right thing always—which is what is best for the organization not themselves. They are charged with doing what is best, and fair for the organization. When you describe what is actually going on, talent hoarding is far from what is right and just and fair for the organization. It is instead what is best and easiest for them.

Allow me to welcome you to a full view of the grand hypocrisy that exists in corporate America regarding talent management. Talent hoarding is alive and well. In fact, it is the norm. It is unusual to find or hear of companies that do this well. But there are some and they are household names.

If you go back and do an assessment, and they really look at it, talent hoarding provides no benefit to an organization. If you think about it, if executives don't want to flow talent because that means in some way they are back to square one, that they've lost one of their key players who will now be in a position to make one of their peers look good. The internal value system is askew. The internal value system should not be where your worth is based upon how well you do. It should instead be based on how well your team does—or basically, how well your team does as a result of your leadership. In my opinion, your value as a leader in corporate America could again be seen through the lens of a professional football analogy.

STUCK IN THE MIDDLE

Bill Parcells is seen as having one of the strongest coaching lineages with the greatest successes as a group in the National Football League. There are quite a few coaches in the National Football League (NFL) who spent time under Parcells. The list includes Bill Belichick, Tom Coughlin, Sean Payton, Charlie Weis, and Romeo Crennel. Each of these coaches who are deemed to be above average coaches in the NFL and each has gone on to be Super Bowl winning coaches. A common factor, they all learned from and were mentored by one man... Bill Parcells.

Why not have these same instances of storied lineage become part of a corporate culture? Joe Smith just made VP? Oh, he used to work for Denise back in the day. Denise is a kingmaker. Everyone who's worked for Denise has done well, moved on to bigger things, and better roles in the company. Now that person has success and Denise's internal stock in the company rises; she becomes a conduit for leadership development within the organization. Denise in turn is branded as having a leadership lineage with deep roots of success as the strongest protégés. And the people coming up under Denise realize that everything is working to everyone's best interests. It's an alignment, a synchronization of things.

You know that your purpose there is to work within the system, because that system works. It's really simple. You spend three years with Denise, and watch what happens. Your career will take off. Gen Xers can sit there and say, "Okay, I will give it three years." Flowing talent, I believe, is the thing that meets the mark in retaining high potentials and slowing the bleed at the senior manager and director level. Flowing talent can reset the Gen Xer three-year plan, and give you more time with that top talent, and an opportunity to successfully retain them as a part of your organization.

A quick way for leaders to determine who to flow is to target an employee who has been deemed high potential two years in a row. As an organizational process they should either be promoted or placed on a glide path into another role within the organization. If they choose not to be so moved, that's fine. A conversation with the individual might sound like this:

"You've been a high potential for two years in a row. What do you want to do in the organization?"

"I want to run a division."

"Really? Which particular division would you like to run?"

"I'd like to go out to the Southwestern division."

"What role would you want?"

"I really want to run Customer Service for the entire Southwestern division."

"Okay, so let's think about this. Where can we put you so that you're in line to be able to do that? Because where you are right now not is not preparing you for that. Where you are right now is not going to get you there. Let's figure this out together. I'll make some calls. The next time we get together one-on-one, we'll talk about how we're going to continue to move towards this. But at the same time, while I'm doing this, I need you to think about who is going to replace you if you go there."

"Yes, I would love to do that. Thanks for being so open to listening to my career aspirations."

This is what true talent management sounds like, feels like, and looks like when you do the right things... always.

CHAPTER TWELVE

Mind The Gap

Nobody knows what is the best he can do.

– Arturo Toscanini

There is a space, a void if you will, between talent management and employee engagement in many organizations. Talent management, as we discussed in the last chapter, should be about four things:

1. Know (the top talented people in the organization)
2. Grow (their knowledge, skills, and abilities to succeed at the next level)
3. Show (their skills to others through opportunities to demonstrate their abilities)
4. Flow (by moving top talent through the organization)

Know who they are, grow them to where they want to be, show their abilities off, and then flow them to where it's best for the organization to help it grow into the role that they want to be in the future and to sustain themselves for who they are today.

In most organizations, employee engagement is a piece that should be firmly rooted in the talent management strategy, and it's not. In fact, for most companies it is not even part of the conversation. When you say talent management to most corporations, they think you're talking about recruiting, which is solely about getting talent in the door. That's a misperception. Recruiting is indeed about attracting talent to the organization. However, it is only one part of an integrated talent management strategy. As a model talent management activity could simply follow three separate acts in the stage of talent management: attract, engage, and retain top talent.

You attract the right talent, keep them engaged and then you'll retain them. Where corporations often flub their lines is in act two of our play: engage–which then raises audience expectations for the final act: retain. Once you get them in you have to determine if they're happy. If they're not happy, you're going to lose them. And you will not retain someone who isn't truly happy or engaged. Well, at least not for very long.

Companies still struggle today with whether or not to tell their high potentials that they are high potentials. Many executives have said, *"If you tell them they're high potentials, they're going to walk around here like they're god's gift to the organization."* That's one school of thought. The other is, *"Tell them they're high potentials so that maybe they will stay around and work towards being someone that the organization needs, because they know that they're valued."*

Speaking from my own experience there was a point where I was ready to leave an organization I worked for not too long ago. My last week in the office, I met with my then boss' boss, who said to me, *"I can't believe we're losing you. You're one of our high potentials."* I replied, *"If I had known that a month ago, and knew what that meant for my future at this company, I might have stayed."* Her jaw hit the floor. I can still see her face. If no one told me that, how was I supposed to know? Being a high potential should not be a guessing game. I am certain that as employees resign from one company for an opportunity at another, they hear this said often. Sadly, a leader having to say this is admitting that they did not do all that they could have done to retain you as top talent.

STUCK IN THE MIDDLE

Often the scenario with organizations is that they don't want to acknowledge the truth. They don't want to tell someone they're high potential because they don't want them to become stuck up. In my opinion, this is not doing the right thing always. You are dropping the ball in my opinion as a leader if you do not take the opportunity to tell them they are valued.

When you've got a person who has potential, who is that rising star, you find a way to work them into your game plan. Bill Belichick of the New England Patriots, to go back to NFL coaching, uses his assets, his players, and his resources better than other coaches. He is noted for how he manages the team's NFL draft picks better—many believe—than any other NFL team. In short, Belichick is a master at managing talent in its most visible sense. He gets drafting new players, and signing free agents right almost every year, and that turns into New England Patriots wins almost every Sunday.

Four little words—know, grow, show, and flow—form a simple checklist for how to properly manage top talent. There is honesty in each of the four simple steps. At the core is the truth of what you know about that talent, the truth of how you grow the skills of that talent, the truth that you show others how talented your people are in terms of their value, and truth in sharing that talent as you flow them through the organization. That's the little thing that most organizations miss out on doing and why they fail at talent management and top talent retention. Eleventh hour talent retention is reactive. It's much like, *"Oh goodness, we better go shut the barn door"* after the horse has already gotten out and is headed down the road. Retention problems are a major cost, and are caused by many smaller, underlying issues. Sometimes it's compensation. Sometimes it's appreciation. Sometimes it's just wrong fit—the role and the person are just not compatible.

But for every little thing that is a component of the problem, there is a way to address it. But you have to be willing to drill down in order to identify what you need to correct in your methodology and approach to talent management and retention.

Here is an example of something that organizations famously do often but don't do well or flat out does it incorrectly. It is known simply as the exit interview.

The exit interview is the de facto link to employee engagement for the departing employees of the organization. HR sits down with someone before their last day with the company and asks the employee ,*"Why are you leaving?"* The person's reply is probably, *"Well, I just had a better opportunity."*

Translation: *"I didn't want to go, but you guys didn't develop me; with this other company I'm getting more money, I'm getting more opportunity—than I got from you. But, I'm not going to burn a bridge, so I'm not going to really tell you anything."*

Another new thing that some organizations now do is tell the now former employee: *"We'll have a third party call you in 30 days and follow up with you."*

Why do they do that?

Because they were afraid that they'd get scathing exit interviews and feel that after 30 days people would be nicer and really tell them the truth. Well, 30 days later, the person is onto their new job and probably has moved past the point of caring about the old organization. The third party asks them,

"Why did you leave?"

"Um, better opportunity."

"Anything you'd like to share with us about the company?"

"Nope."

"Would you work for the organization again?"

"Um, sure."

They each hang up the phone.

Nothing is gained by conducting exit interviews.

Here is what I think the organization should do instead. To many it is known as the stay interview. Stay interview could give you specifics on what you, as an organization, need to focus on continuing to do or if there is some leverage to propose to stop doing something that is not working well.

Why don't you talk to select talented employees who have stayed with the company for some period of time (at least over three years) and ask them, *"Why are you staying with this organization?"* Every quarter, ask that same question, *"Why are you staying?"* And you'll get answers that will be more helpful to you when it comes to retention. *"Well, because I like (X) and I like (Y) about the company, my boss, and my peers."*

You've got a better chance of getting a true picture of things every quarter from people who are staying than from those who leave. When they leave, they aren't obligated to tell you anything of value. When they are staying, they might be honest and say, *"I'm really happy here."* Or *"Things would be better here if this were to change."*

A stay interview is a tangible, tactical practice that organizations overlook.

Connect with those employees you deem to be high potentials, those employees who you know are critical that you can't live without in the organization, those employees with the "never out" jobs and ask them:

"You've been here for fifteen years, and we love the fact that you have chosen to stay with us. Why have you stayed?"

"I am putting four kids through college and I've got one more to go. Then I'm retiring."

You will get answers like this but you will also probably get people to tell you:

"I like it here; I like my boss; I like my coworkers; I like the short commute to work every day; my mom works here; I identify with the company mission."

Think how much more powerful the information from a stay interview will be than from an exit interview—where you've got no upside. An exit interview is either going to be negative, or it's going to be neutral. Neither option is going to help you. How powerful is the stay interview? You get a lucid look at your organization. It's far superior to the employee engagement survey, which I think is useless. Nothing like a targeted survey that uses leading questions to illicit a palatable, more favorable response or data set that can be used to show at least a concern for employee morale.

Employee engagement surveys—are supposedly done anonymously but I've been part of HR long enough to know that they are only "anonymous" from the standpoint that the employees didn't put their name on it. But any HR executive with savvy can cut and slice the responses and say,

"I want to look at all director and above leaders in HR in Philadelphia within this segment of the organization in this building on this floor. Gee, there are only three of them. Okay, of those people, who seems to be the most disgruntled? That guy. Well, we know who said the negative things. Let's watch that guy closely for the next six months."

They could be wrong about who said what, but think about it—that's not anonymous—and it does happen, the "figuring out whose survey is this." I've been in meetings where other executives have said, *"We're going to narrow down on that part of the organization. We want to understand how they really feel."* So again, they are going to precisely focus on a group of people easily identifiable even from an "anonymous" survey?

The bottom line when it comes to employee engagement surveys is that people are afraid to be themselves, just like with the exit interview. They are afraid of burning bridges. They are afraid of retribution. They are afraid of being seen as not a team player. All of these fears create an inability or reluctance for employees to truly be themselves at work. Employers become indifferent to telling the truth in the employee engagement survey because they know nothing's going to change. What can organizations do instead?

Save the money spent on employee engagement surveys.

Every other year organizations try to find out if they are doing what they should be doing for their employees, and if their employees are happy. Instead, they get minimal truth in the information and that doesn't allow companies to do anything actionable to make improvements in the business or institute better treatment of the employee population. By the time the organization gets around to making the changes asked for or recommended by the employees as a result from the survey, it is conveniently time for the next survey and not enough time to make change. I have actually been a part of organizations that would skip the administration of a scheduled survey because they did not want to hear bad news (the truth) from employees about the true state of the organization. They postponed the survey because they hadn't done anything with the last information collected. They postponed the truth, they postponed taking real action–but they foolishly expected that employee engagement would increase simply because they asked about it in the survey. This organization is like many others. They are not unique and their miscues with this tool are common. But I think there is a simple alternative to this folly.

Assess employee engagement quarterly using a stay interview of top talent.

Anything longer than that is not in synch with the conventional reporting system for many large organizations. If the survey is done every year or every other year, you've missed timely opportunities to act on the results from the pursuit of identifying areas to fix. If stay interviews are done quarterly, you've got an opportunity to do something, to gauge it, to assess it, to utilize it for the next quarter or maybe two quarters out, so you're not losing the benefit of acting on what you can determine. By utilizing the positives of the stay interview you gain the ability to play to your strengths forward and that can make a tangible impact within each quarter of the calendar/fiscal year. Two groups within the employee population that you should be talking to every quarter are those who have been deemed to be high potential—because that's a finite group—and then there are the "criticals."

I have to make a side step here to explain who the "criticals' are and why they matter. I was with one organization where they termed key employees as CPIKs. It's an acronym for Critical Persons with Institutional Knowledge. Who are those critical persons, or employees with deep or unique institutional knowledge? They come from the population who are holders of the before mentioned "never out" jobs. An example of a CPIK is Jack down in accounting. He is the only one with the company who still knows how use the legacy accounting software, and understandings the paper-based filing system. If Jack's not there, who is going to save our butts the next time we get audited? Jack then, in my opinion, should be the first person contacted for a stay interview.

Now someone might read these last two paragraphs and say, *"This guy's out of his mind. There's no way we're going to survey all 50,000 people in our organization every quarter."* I'm not suggesting that. What I am suggesting is that with a little planning, over a year (four quarters) that you could talk to each high potential or CPIK at least once.

At a bare minimum, proactive organizations that are committed to talent management could implement a policy for quarterly stay interviews of their HiPos and CPIKs. Even if that comes to a hundred people it's worth it. You only need to ask them three questions at the most:

1. Why have you stayed with our organization?
2. What would be a cause for you to leave our organization?

3. What should we do (start, stop, or continue) to retain you with our organization?

That's it. Ask those three questions every quarter and document the answers as given from each HiPo and CPIK. Now at the end of the year you can trend it out. Supposed you trended the answer to the question of *"What would be a cause for you to leave our organization?"* and discovered that the most popular answer was if the organization ever closed the on-site daycare, many talented people would need to look elsewhere for employment? If you see that reason repeatedly then you know something for certain– that you can expect job vacancies from many of your HiPos and CPIKs if you ever close the on-site daycare.

Playing that forward, let's say you're in a budget meeting, and someone proposes that to cut cost, the organization should eliminate the on-site daycare center. By using the data from the quarterly stay interviews of your top talent, you can argue against this option with a high degree of confidence and certainty that continuing with that decision will have repercussions. Bring that out in the meeting, *"We need to figure out an alternative or we could lose a lot of good people if we don't find another option."*

If you know you need to make cuts, then you know to look elsewhere, you know now to find somewhere else to cut back on spending, to find another option that will not have such a negative impact on the top talent you are looking to keep. Simply by closing the on-site daycare you could leave many of your employees stuck in the middle between caring for their family, and working for your organization.

CHAPTER THIRTEEN

Talent Management Geometry

Our real problem is not our strength today; it is rather the vital necessity of action today to ensure our strength tomorrow.

— Calvin Coolidge

When you're talking about manifesting what could be a cultural change in an organization—not a quick fix but a change that takes time—that's not something you can do from the ground up. If the top leader doesn't believe in it, it doesn't matter how much you do at the bottom, because it's not going to be sustainable. Employees aren't going to buy into it because the leadership above them doesn't. In an ideal company in an ideal world, you would have folks at the top saying,

"This is something that we now fundamentally need to change about our organization so we don't run it into situations like we've been in in the past, where we've had to lay of thousands of people or completely gut part of our business just to stay viable. We need to do something that allows us to have a viable talent management model, which helps have a sustainable workforce, to be optimal, to have that right balance between numbers of employees, managers, and senior leaders... the sweet spot for our business, for our organization."

The only way that you can do that, so it isn't just another tail-chasing expedition—is to get the top executive to buy into it and say, *"It starts here with me as the CEO and flows down from me."* Because when it starts at the top, people underneath are going to take it seriously. If you start it at the lowest level, at the first layer of supervision, that's not going to work. It will become another corporate fire drill where senior leadership will politely pass the buck to lower level employees through delegation so they can quickly push it off their desk. That's exactly what happens in many organizations.

There are however some enlightened corporations that don't think or act that way. They have tremendously strong, profitable organizations. And they're different than any other organization because they're willing to advocate for integrated talent management as the way that they look at their organization and this way of seeing their company makes their

The most innovative, powerful, inspiring organizations are those companies that know themselves. They know their talented people. They are comfortable in their own skin. They have to be comfortable with their own way of doing things, which may be different than what they read about in The Wall Street Journal. It may be different than what Forbes magazine says, or differs with some pundit's opinion of the way business should be done.

Not every organization is the same. Even organizations within the exact same industry don't run their business like their competitors. You don't have to follow someone else's model of how it's done—it is monolithic, it is structured. When you push your way of operating down to the lowest common denominator and homogenize it, you lose everything unique or that which gives you competitive difference. You lose everything that goes to making your company viable in your market or industry. You become just like someone else.

As an example, how many leaders have gone out and tried to implement Six Sigma in their organization because all their competitors "are doing it" and had it fail miserably because it doesn't fit the corporate culture? It was like that some years ago with ISO9000 (Statistical Process Control). Consultant's made millions in the late 1990s getting organizations ISO9000 certified. Do companies even focus on it anymore? Does it even matter? Everyone wants a one-size-fits-all solution. It appeals to the masses. A lot of people will buy it. They will think we can do this or buy this and implement it and we're done... no more problems. Remember there is no magic button that you can push and not any magic pill you can swallow. (Regardless of what the numerous infomercials at 3:00am would have you believe.)

To find solutions that work you have to understand your own organization, understand your assets and your resources. And I'm not about talking equipment such as how many printing presses, copy machines, or heavy machines you have for spitting out fabricated parts. It's about the individuals that run those machines or provide service to your customers. That's the asset that generates your business for you; it's the people. When you acknowledge at the top that the way you've done things in the past is flawed, then you have an opportunity to fix things. There are certainly bright CEOs and boards of directors that now realize, *"We can't go back to doing things the way we've always done them, because we'll end up going in a circle."* That's what many call a "doom loop."

Leaders and senior executives must be willing to do that honest assessment and drive that change from the top. That means starting to ask, *"Why do you stay here?" "What would lure you away?"* That will be the key to you flowing your talent all the way through your organization and to finding out what works and what doesn't.

One of my favorite talent management stories is the particulars of the succession plan for Jack Welch at GE. When Jack Welch was ready to step down from being the CEO of GE, he already had identified three people that he would groom to replace him: Immelt, McNerney, and Nardelli. They all had their opportunity to be the next CEO of GE. Not one guy, three guys. When Welch picked Immelt, what happened to the other two guys? They left immediately. McNerney went to 3M. Nardelli went to Home Depot. Why did they leave? I suspect that both leaders felt that being second place was being the first loser. And, to add insult to injury, they would be staying on with an organization where their new boss was formerly their peer and fierce rival for the top spot.

What Jack Welch did that was genius was he made sure that he had three suitors for his role. He applied proactive talent management in the form of succession planning so that there was top talent ready under him. The example of talent management was started and practiced in full view of those in the organization. That's why GE has long been respected for being a well-run talent management focused organization.

Top Down or Groundswell Approach

The challenge organizations run into is that you can do talent management two ways: Top down, or Groundswell.

Groundswell talent management does not work. Thinking or saying, *"Look, the employees in the organization will manage their talent themselves."* I've not seen groundswell talent management work as well as it does and did for social media. It doesn't do anything to take away from the "mine, mine, mine" practice of talent hoarding I mentioned earlier that some leaders employ. Again, here's how that theory translates to those watching; *"I don't want you to know how good my senior manager is, because if I give him to you, I'm screwed. He makes me look good and if he goes I am worried (insecure) about myself. It's got nothing to do about my loyalty or care for the organization. I'm worried about me and if I can still look good without him on my team."*

In my experience, this happens all too often and is one of the major reasons the groundswell approach doesn't work... because of fear.

The top down approach has flaws too that often cause failure—it fails because it is missing a component. However, this is an easier, and quicker to fix than the deeper culture change needed to address issues with the groundswell approach. The top in this instance is the Board of Directors. The Board says, *"We need talent management. We need a succession plan. We need a workforce plan."* Why you may ask is this a concern or the Board of Directors?

Because the Board cares about one thing: that the company continues to make money so it can stay profitable, so they can stay on the Board. Guess what? The way you do that is to make sure the organization is well run when it comes to people, processes, finances, and serving customers to name a few aspects. They lean on the CEO to make sure that all that happens.

Every Board has at least one meeting of the directors every year that looks at the talent management, diversity, inclusion, and all HR facets. That HR meeting is where they sit and try to make sure they have the right people, that there's a succession plan for key leaders. They want to see some type of plan for *"If this person leaves, who is their replacement? If that person leaves, who is their replacement?"* Notice I kept using the word replacement. That's because most organizations do not practice succession planning; they instead practice replacement planning. They are masters of being reactionary.

What happens when you get to the place when there's no one internally ready to put in an open position, into a "never out" job?

"We have got to hire somebody." On most levels, that makes sense. But here is where talent management from the top down begins to fail. The CEO understands the need for talent management. He or she has to, because they're getting kicked hard from the Board of Directors. *"We need talent management to make sure we've got the best people."* *"We got it, it makes sense to us. We'll execute on it."* The CEO gets it, because the CEO is thinking, *"Okay, I've got three EVPs working for me. If one of these three leaves, I know who's in the replacement stack."*

However, if one of their direct reports of the EVP leaves, *"We don't have anybody so we would have to hire from outside."* At the top, the CEO's may have their successors. Underneath, each EVP has their team of key people one of which may be a successor. That's about it. It's very shallow. We are looking at 15 to 20 people in the roles of EVP, SVP, or as the direct and extended direct report executive level complement to the CEO. It would be easy to think that only these employees "matter" in the organization. Sadly, this is typical and why most think of succession planning as being something done only for the most senior executives.

The reason why talent management breaks down is because under this group of 15 to 20 people–the VPs and senior directors–they don't know how to do talent management. Nobody has ever shown them how. There's a gap and it exists mostly because SVPs and up don't know it exists. The reason it exists is because when it comes to talent management you can't delegate it. You have to take ownership every step of the way. There is a certain amount of responsibility at every level to make sure that it is done.

That's the piece that's missing. If there's a responsibility for talent management at any level, there should be a playbook, a work package, something that says, "Talent Management Responsibilities." In that playbook there should also be how you'll be measured against those responsibilities based upon your performance as leader.

Simplistically put, a fix that I have seen work is to discover either internally or through some outside consultative guidance that a void exists, and create talent management responsibilities playbook for your first-level executives and senior managers. Basically any leader with direct reports in an organization should have the playbook... and be shown how to use it.

But there's a level of resistance to this. Resistance because it is not *"How we do things around here."* So the challenge becomes how do you remove the resistance and give leaders the tools to make it work, and also hold them accountable with measurement? A system to say, *"This is how you identify and lead top talent,"* so that everyone knows this is what's expected, this is how I do it, and this is how I'm going to be measured. John D. Rockefeller said this, *"What you can measure, you can improve."* I would add to that the phrase the familiar sentiment that whatever gets measured in the public gets done in private.

What are the metrics? What are we measuring to show them, *"yes, you are on track"* or *"no, you are not on track."* There are plenty of things that are out there that can be utilized. Many employees don't like the word "metric" because it conjures up visions of torture to people who don't like to be graded and evaluated. But you can create a check list where, as a metric each leader is charged with flowing a pre-determined percentage of their high-potentials, or critical point of institutional knowledge employees to positions of greater responsibility and seniority in the organization every one or two years.

There has to be a demonstrable effort made by each leader (manager or executive) who is charged with growing talent in the organization. It can't just simply be promoting. It has to be, *"What are they doing? Are they giving this person stretch assignments? What are they doing to give this person exposure? How are they managing that?"*

In effect, I am saying you cannot simply rely on a centralized talent management function. You need to do more than just have one talent management guru within the organization as the coordinator of all talent management efforts within the organization. Each leader should also be charged, taught, and measured on the importance of managing the talent in their organization. This is not a reversal of the opinion as discussed earlier where one person alone is responsible to wear the yoke of organizational change. I am instead advocating for this champion be supported by a "coalition of the willing" in place to help that individual and who that individual in turn helps.

STUCK IN THE MIDDLE

Top talent is all about of rise over run, and an inverted letter "L".

As mentioned briefly to this point, most companies use the 9-Box grid system. The whole idea behind the 9-Box grid is it's based on rise over run around two aspects: potential and performance. There's performance—what I can see you do, what projects you've done. There's potential—the things I think you can do, the jobs that I want to give you a shot at, the roles I think you can aspire to.

Box 9 is a destination both high on the X-axis, and high on the Y-axis. If I am in Box 9, I am high potential and I am high performance. People in that box are the ready bench, the future leaders of the organization. These should be the rare few that I want to hold onto in my organization at all costs. They do a lot of work; they've got great potential to be even more than they are right now. There should be names in this box that are known to everyone in the organization.

In Box 8, you will find people who are really high on their potential but maybe their performance is not as high as it could be. They are very important people in the organization but might need coaching, some mentoring, and different assignments to raise their level of performance.

Over in Box 7, I've got somebody high potential but their performance might be low. Maybe they are new, not to the organization but perhaps in the role, but maybe they are in a growth curve, or they're really struggling right now with their performance. They need more coaching, more mentoring, and maybe more direction.

Box 6, this person is a doer. That's the bottom line. They are a doer. We want to keep them. They get a lot of stuff done. Their potential is solid to complement their hard work.

Box 5, is someone who is medium performance and they're medium potential. Steady Eddy or Steady Betty here is that middle manager, the person you really need and depend on who gets the work done.

Box 4 is visible as you look down through the stack to the medium aspect, somebody who is medium potential but low performance. What are you doing for this person? What things are in this box to help move them out of here? This is all about getting this person to show more potential while working hard on their low performance. To increase their performance; you've got to coach them.

Box 3, someone is a really high performer but they're low in potential. Again, this person is a doer. They might just be a person who is the whole salt of the earth. A needed cog that may never become a big wheel.

Box 2, this person has medium performance, low potential. What do we do to get them up high performance? Maybe they don't have any potential because they don't want to be anything more than they are.

Box 1 is low potential and low performance. Someone ends up here the first time, you try to coach, mentor, or help them get out of that box. If they end up there a second time, you have to get them out of the organization.

So you evaluate your 9-Box grid. You've got two doers over here. You've got someone who is holding steady. You've got this person here as up and coming. Then you've got your high potentials. And you've got the marginal that if they can't move to a higher box—they have to be let go.

9-Box Grid Theoretical/Recommended Use

The performance and potential matrix (9-Box grid) is one the best talent management tools I've ever used. Allow me to share a brief tutorial on how I have seen this tool used best:

What is it?

The matrix is used to evaluate an organization's talent pool. Here's the basic format:
The X-axis (horizontal line) of 3 boxes assesses leadership performance and the Y-axis of 3 boxes (vertical line) assesses leadership potential. A combination of Y and X-axis makes up the box within the grid that the leader is placed.

Why use it?

1. It's a simple way to assess any population of leaders on two important dimensions
2. It's a great way to facilitate a dialog amongst a senior leadership team. Teams use it to calibrate their expectations and ratings
3. With a good open debate, the multiple perspectives provide for a much more accurate assessment (vs. one person's opinion) of talent
4. The process can facilitate a shared sense of ownership for the organizations talent pool of top talent

5. It's a great way to identify development needs and transition to development planning

How to use it-

The tool is best if used by a team and facilitated by someone who has experience with the process. This could be an HR person, OD consultant, or someone responsible for leadership development or succession planning. You should present the tool and process to the team to make sure they all understand and buy into the purpose and process. Don't underestimate the amount of anxiety you will encounter if a team has never done anything like this (a ranking exercise) before.

It's best to decide ahead of time how performance will be assessed (use a leadership competency model if you have one) and how potential will be assessed. You could also ask for any other relevant information, such as years in current position, diversity status, retention risk, or ability/willingness to relocate. I usually have each manager plot their direct report managers (one level at a time, so we're comparing apples to apples) and send their completed grid to me. I then consolidate all of the names on to one grid. Either as part of a multi-day off-site meeting where I bring copies of the consolidated grid and facilitate the discussion.

It's easier selecting someone in Box 1 (lowest performance and potential) where you think there may be very little disagreement, than it will be to select someone in Box 9 (highest performance and potential) where they will be many opinions. Ask the sponsor or manager to explain the rationale for either assessment. Ask why, ask for supporting examples often, and invite all others to comment. Don't rush it; the benefit of this process is in the discussion. After all have been heard from, if there is agreement, then you have a benchmark for all others to compare against. If there is disagreement in perception, ask the sponsor manager if they want to change their mind based on the feedback – usually they do – but if not, leave it. Pick another name until you establish the benchmark. You can then discuss rest of the names in the Box 9, then move to the bordering boxes (Box 6 and Box 8). Then move to the Box 7, and again, facilitate a dialog to establish another benchmark. Continue the discussion for each person. For succession planning, the focus should be on the upper right hand corner boxes (Boxes 6, 8, and 9) – this is your high potential pool... graphically this is shown as the "inverted L" and where you should focus first. I am not saying to only focus on this group, but to know that this is the best practice target area for pools of top talent.

Follow-up on a quarterly basis to monitor development plans. Repeat the assessment process at least once a year. The next section is abridged on purpose as I am only presenting here what we will discuss later. However, it is complete enough to contain a full version of the 9-Box Grid and a set of descriptions to be used with each box as a tool for organizations; at the same time it is streamlined enough to be a tutorial for individuals who wish to better understand this mysterious process that is often made invisible to them as employees of organizations.

9-Box Grid Box Definition / Recommended Development Actions

High Potential/Low Performance (7)	High Potential/Medium Performance (8)	High Potential/High Performance (9)
Medium Potential/Low Performance (4)	Medium Potential/Medium Performance (5)	Medium Potential/High Performance (6)
Low Potential/Low Performance (1)	Low Potential/Medium Performance (2)	Low Potential/High Performance (3)

POTENTIAL / PERFORMANCE

1. PROBLEM PERFORMER

DEFINITION: Is not delivering on expected results in current role. Future with the company uncertain.

ACTION: If low performance is due to job fit, reassign. If low performance is due to ability or motivation, person should be removed from position or should be coached to full performance within a reasonable period of time.

2. SPECIAL ATTENTION

DEFINITION: Performance falls short in current job, but shows promise for a different type of role, or may be a new position not yet mastered.

ACTION: If not already on counseling, create a performance improvement plan and/or create exit plan.

3. **N/A**

   DEFINITION: New to organization (< 6 months) and is moving up the learning curve.

   ACTION: Assimilate into the firm and role. Clearly convey job expectations. Accelerate time-to-performance

4. **WELL PLACED**

   DEFINITION: Delivers on expectations in the current role and is probably capable of performing effectively in another role of similar scope.

   ACTION: Continue to develop in role. Coach, reward and encourage

5. **DEVELOP**

   DEFINITION: Delivers on expectations in current role. May be relatively new in position and still growing into job.

   ACTION: Coach, reward and encourage. Likely promotable in 2-3 years.

6. **HIGH PERFORMER**

   DEFINITION: Delivers on expectations. Meeting objectives & contributing in role. (we will add to this definition)

   ACTION: Coach, reward and encourage. Promotable to next level within 1-3 years and possibly beyond in long term.

7. **HIGH PROFESSIONAL**

   DEFINITION: Consistently exceeds expectations. An expert who is of great value to the company.

   ACTION: Utilize as a role model and resident expert. Actively retain. Recognize contributions and reward

8. **HIGH POTENTIAL**

   DEFINITION: Consistently exceeds expectations. Has mastered most if not all aspects of current role and is ready for a new challenge to broaden experience.

ACTION: Consider lateral movements, stretch assignments or cross-functional projects. Coach, reward & encourage

9. **FUTURE LEADER**
DEFINITION: Consistently exceeds expectations. Has mastered all aspects of current role. Strong performer with the possibility for promotion.
ACTION: Promote to higher band within 12 months. Identify ready now successors

Supporting Specifics

The setup to using the 9-Box grid was numerous meetings with senior leaders from the lines of business; I was able to drill down to the one key business imperative that keeps them up at night.

That imperative takes the form of a question that haunts them by asking is the line of business they lead prepared for the business imperatives of tomorrow with the talent of today? The 9-Box grid serves as a roadmap and our visual planned route of how we can arrive at an organization that deploys human capital at the right time, in the right place, and with the right knowledge, skills, and abilities.

Most leaders are committed to this thought process. But that commitment must be shared by leaders who need expert help in the areas discussed as talent levers. That commitment is the foundation of a high performance culture. It is by purposefully engaging these levers in proper process that will drive behavior change within the organization. And to complete the process change, we can look forward to see that we are now closer to the biggest imperative in these challenging times ... changing the culture with respect to talent management to support the organization's strategic direction.

When I mention promote here, it is the idea of promoting talent growth and movement not necessarily moving to a higher positional role Specifically, this strategy must at any time in the career progression of employees give them a line of sight that illustrates how they progress through the organization. This end-to-end look at talent management is new for many organizations. The benefit to us all is that it will provide us for the first time a toolkit for how to know, grow, show, and finally flow talent though the organization.

The 9-Box Grid is helpful in as this identifies the employees in the inverted "L" that are demonstrating the levels of performance and potential we hope to see in all employees in a high performance culture.

The added value of using a tool such as this is that it also allows us to identify the specific needs of all our employees and pinpoint our talent development actions to assist them increasing their levels of performance and opportunities to demonstrate their fullest potential.

From a workforce planning perspective, this 9-Box grid gives us a snapshot of the type of talent we both have and need in the organization. It is this type of proactive inventory that allows a talent management strategy to exist. Identifying the talent we have is the first and most important step in managing the talent of the organization and sets the stage for how we will as mentioned earlier flow talent through the organization.

Since its development, the 9-Box grid has been used by companies seeking an easier way to identify potential successors to the top roles. Part of the attraction is the model's simplicity, which, in theory, arranges every employee into one of nine, neat boxes based on three ratings of performance and three of potential. Assessing along the performance axis is something that companies generally do well – the challenge comes from accurately assessing along the potential axis.

A common mistake that companies make is to assume that strong past performance means that a person has high potential for the future. Making that jump is often a mistake, for a number of reasons; not the least because observing people in their current roles does not guarantee that they will be seen exhibiting the characteristics and behaviors required in more senior roles.

HiPos have three characteristics–ability, aspiration, and engagement. This means that they are capable–bright, fast learners, who can adapt to new job situations and responsibilities. They are motivated, ambitious, and hungry for more responsibility. They are dedicated, and their loyalty to the company and where it is going shows easily. They are flexible, able to move into new roles and adapt to the changing demands of their organization.

Although Gen Xers with all of these characteristics–and a healthy dose of leadership qualities–will likely reach senior levels in most organizations, there is no one size fits all definition. High-potential talent means different things to different organizations and it must be defined in the context of the organizational objectives and culture of each organization.

Any program designed to evaluate HiPos must give people a real opportunity to demonstrate behaviors and capabilities beyond their current role, even if that is through a special project, or trying different job roles to which they appear better suited. It is important to remember that not all employees are natural leaders–those high achievers might have the potential to add value to the organization in an influential technical role. These employees are often referred to as core talent and, while they may have the potential to develop into jobs with greater responsibility; they are likely to do so over a longer period of time than those destined for senior leadership roles.

HiPo development programs are, as a best practice, tailored to ensure that each individual can be managed to ensure that they give their best, and this can only happen if the company is really aware of the difference between past performance and future potential.

* * *

How then is potential easily identified?

The 9-Box Grid is a visual framework that can assist leaders in making their determinations as to which of their employees have both a demonstrated and expressed examples of ability, aspiration, and engagement.

I would identify HiPos as those who both (1) demonstrate and (2) express their ability, aspiration, and engagement. When you have both demonstrated and expressed these three characteristics—you've now got six lenses to focus with on those deemed to be top talent.
If somebody is in the high-potential / high-performance box, Box 9, they should have a high degree of each attribute as both demonstrated and expressed. Gen Xers can see it and they're talking about it. They're highly able to do the job. They're extremely engaged. They have a high ambition to be the next

biggest whatever. Top talent has all six check marks. You have to have all six to get into Box 9.

If you've got five out of the six—let's say you have demonstrated and expressed ability, (two check marks) and engagement (two more check marks), but you haven't demonstrated that you have the aspiration to move to the next level ... you might be talking about it (one more check mark) but you're not demonstrating it—to me, that automatically takes you out of being in Box 9 and puts you in Box 8. The fewer of these maximum of six check marks you have, and depending of course on which ones are absent, the more I target through practical experience where you should be in this grid. I match the check marks to the boxes as a method to create a focused development for each employee using their 9-Box grid placement as the foundation to a robust career progression discussion.

So, if Tom was in Box 6, he would be considered medium potential but high performance as both demonstrated and expressed. Maybe Tom is demonstrating and expressing my ability and engagement, but Tom is not acting or talking about wanting to take on any more responsibility or move higher in the organization than he is now. That's an absence of demonstrated or expressed ambition and not a high potential in my book. That's somebody who is outside of the high-potential box. But, this person might be one of our before mentioned CPIKs that we need to hold onto. So what do we do? When we talk about the stay interviews, we need to target boxes 6, 8, and 9. Focusing in on the inverted L, this is again where the organization should spend most of their time on developing their bench strength for the future. Maybe Tom as mentioned above is in Box 6, but they could certainly move somewhere else in the "inverted L" formed by neighboring Box 8.

How do we get these people to be where they want to be and continue to move them through? Not everybody should or even wants to be moving toward the "inverted L". For those that find themselves placed in Box 6, they should not be disillusioned to what this means. We (and they) need to understand what that means for them and the role they play. And they need to understand that that's where we are assessing their role to be. Here are an example of what dialog with a HiPos placed in each of the boxes of the inverted L might sound like:

Box 6

"You never really talk about wanting to be a director."

"I don't want to do that job. I don't want to carry a Blackberry. I don't want work to be like that. I love what I do. I just want to keep doing it."

"Perfect! So why do you stay? What would lure you away? And what do I need to do to make sure that that never happens?"

"Just keep giving me the projects you've been giving me. I really love the fact that I can work from home on Fridays. Every once in a while, I'd like to work on a cross-functional project."

Box 8

"What do you need from me as you leader, and how can I help?"

"Where I am right now, I need to take some time. I've got too many things to juggle. I've got too much on my plate."

"Okay, what do we need to take off your plate? What would make the most sense for you?"

"If I didn't have to wash windows every Thursday that would allow me to do this. Or, if I could work from home one day a week and just focus. Get all my conference calls done on one day."

"Okay, let's try that and see what happens."

<u>Box 9</u>

"What do you need from me as you leader, and how can I help?"

"I'm good."

"You've been here for two years in this role. What's next for you?"

"I really want to do lead a cross-functional project team."

"Okay, let's put in place a six-month plan to get you to a place where either (A) you can be that, or you're next in line."

"Oh, I would like that."

"But don't slip up! Because when you do, they will come looking for me."

Here's a critical thing to remember when employing the 9-Box grid process in an organization that is often overlooked. If you take somebody who is a Box 9 high potential as a news reporter and you promote them to news editor, don't expect them to be in Box 9 again immediately. They may fall back two boxes. They may fall down to the bottom row of the 9-Box grid. Go into this conversation, realizing this fact and let the person know that, *"You're going to be doing something you've never done before, so we're going to expect you to have some challenges. That's part of your growth."*

What you don't want to do is to take somebody who is a Box 9, give them a new opportunity and allow them to fail, and become demoralized. If you really believe that this person is a high potential, and you really believe that given the opportunity to grow into the role, then realize that it will take time, months or even years, before they get to a Box 9 in this new position. You've got to give them the opportunity as well as the support. At the first instance of them not doing something right, you can't say or think they shouldn't be in that role.

* * *

In a nutshell, I believe there is an issue that exists between talent management and the learning and development is a simple one. When you're in any box, there should be an associated learning and development objectives to introduce or sustain your movement.

There should be a mix of blended opportunities that goes back to that 70-20-10 model. Challenging assignments, coaching and mentoring, and coursework that gets you in a position where you have the proclivity to move to the next box. Gen Xers should feel that the organization is going to empower and enable them. Unfortunately, most organizations do not do that. They say that they do but they really don't. They say it because they think if they say it that will make their employees happy believe they really do it. They place people in these boxes and often leave them stuck in the middle searching for a way out. That is of course if they even know they are stuck.

CHAPTER FOURTEEN

The difference between talent management and HR

Hard work spotlights the character of people: some turn up their sleeves, some turn up their noses, and some don't turn up at all.

— Sam Ewing

In corporate America, leaders and executives often forget that their leadership objective is not only to manage the company processes, or to supervise the production of widgets. Their role is essentially made important by their charge to lead people. As executives tasked with running a company that is a fundamental and critical component of business that you cannot push off or delegate and expect that someone else has it covered.

Most executives consider talent management a Human Resources (HR) function and as such, best left to the tactical leaders in HR because it is part of their duties to support the company in that effort. The truth is that for talent management to be pervasive and effective in an organization, the primary responsibility should be placed in the hands of the direct managers of employees. Most companies don't formally expect this of their managers and executives so it's not surprising that they just don't do it, and don't know how to do it. This goes back to the need to create a talent management responsibility handbook mentioned earlier.

That's why it's important for organizations to realize this and make a change in what tasks with respect to talent management are the responsibilities of management. Innovative companies that thrive and grow, have leaders at all levels that know they are responsible not just for managing their budget and numbers, but also for the people that work for them—understanding where each person is in their development, and how to best either keep them engaged in their current position, allow them to be seen as that key person in the role, productive for the good of the company, or prepare them so that they can flow to the next level.

When you get to be a senior director, or VP, in my opinion, your job should be focused on helping to build the bench strength of the organization. And that starts with your own team. If you are a leader, your primary job focus should be leading people. That cannot be seen as less important than balancing the department budget. You are on the front line managing the talent of the organization.

Let's go back to the 70-20-10 model. If you are a leader, your work breakdown should match the development percentage mix. You should be spending 70% of your time developing your people by giving them challenging assignments, spending 20% of your time on coaching and mentoring them around both tasks and behaviors, and spending 10% of your time ensuring that they received the needed training to be effective in their jobs, or growing their knowledge through learning and development.

In reality, in many organizations it's the other way around. I know this from my own experience. At one organization, I spent seventy percent of my time doing administrative work, twenty percent coaching and mentoring people, and ten percent leading them—because I was told that by doing my administrative work I would be seen by those people as a good leader. That's not how it should or did work in my opinion. I was instead seen by my direct reports as the executive whipping boy, jerked around by my leader and forced to do tactical work outside of my area of expertise that I was hired for. Regardless of what the job description read, or what I was told in multiple interviews, this was not a leadership role. I was being mismanaged as a high potential, as top talent. I found myself seeing all the classic signs of being stuck in the middle. I was stuck between the job I was hired to do, and the role I was being allowed to play. I did not stay stuck for long. A confluence of circumstances helped me make up my mind and served as a roadmap out of the valley mentioned before... or in this case, out of a valley of despair.

Talent management needs to be seen as every leader's responsibility and they need to be equipped with how to manage that talent. They need to know (or be shown) what that effort looks like in the context of their organization remembering that each organization is unique. A set of metrics could be established so leaders understand that this is important to the organization. Here's a scenario to give some thought to:

At one organization, at the end of each year, they do a survey of the direct reports of each Director and above to find out how well they feel that they've been managed by their leader through the year to come up with a fair overall assessment. And that becomes twenty-five percent of the leader's bonus structure. That is taking talent management seriously. That is the point when the leader would see talent management as their responsibility and to not push it off as, *"That's not my job, that's HR's responsibility."*

No—it is your responsibility. You need to change your effort from being a 70% doer of tasks, to being a leader for 70% and a mentor and a coach for another 20%. Using straight addition, 90% of your time should be developing the current bench for the future needs of the organization. That's talent management.

You may have noticed by now that I believe so strongly in leadership and talent management that leaders should have their compensation tied to doing it well. Every initiative that has worked or been supported in the organizations where I have worked was because it was tied to compensation or bonus percentage payouts. Hitting people in the wallet is sometimes the only way to change a tough organizational culture for the better.

Talent management is not hiring the best and brightest and expecting that because they are so talented that they will just figure it out. It is not allowing someone to fail at a meeting a leader's expectations because the leader was too busy to share what those expectations are upfront. Talent management is not letting an employee feel isolated because the rest of the team speaks a language that no one shares with the new employee. Truly talented people have options. And those options when exercised see those talented people depart your organization. Not for more money, but for greater appreciation of their talent. They leave for greater "civility and respect" from another employer.

The cost it takes to make this realization and drive this truth through the organization is far less than the money flying out of the revolving door of hiring and losing people. I'm not saying this model will preclude a company from ever having to hire talent from the outside, because the business is going to change over time and that might be required. But continuing to hire from the outside while never taking time to assess their internal talent management resources, creates an environment where Gen Xers in the organization believe they don't have any future with the organization, and they start looking elsewhere.

* * *

In any organization, if you only have islands of leaders doing this, it never works. You can't have pockets of opportunity, where only a few executives doing the right thing when it comes to talent management of their direct reports because the whole culture within the company becomes fractured.

As an example, everyone wants to go work for Jane, because Jane does the right thing for her people. But Bill is not skilled as a developer of people. Overall all it's a huge failure because you don't have that integration; you don't have everyone firing on all cylinders. The potential is never realized for the organization. Every organization has stars. Jane is a leader, she brings people along, and this reputation will be a benefit to her brand as someone who streams talented people through the organization. Maybe the people that have been moved through the organization as products of Jane's leadership continue their performance. Maybe they also then become mini-Janes. Maybe they see they are so unique, they depart the organization for greater appreciation of their talent. But, if you've got the disciples of Bill in your organization that aren't leaving, that's the drag coefficient; that's the limiting factor and weak link in the organization.

And it's happening in most companies. When you ask CEOs *"What are their organizations suffering from?"* The issues of poor talent management and lack of leadership bench strength are among the most frequently mentioned issues. As organizations continue to get flatter and try to do more with less, they expect their HR professionals to handle all aspects of the culture change. This is not an HR function, but it is a related function. When you look at the HR generalist, this is not what they're charged with. The HR generalist is supposed to know enough about talent management and recruiting to be able to have a basic conversation. There is a reason they are called "generalists" ... because they are not specialists. And to that matter, the general functions of HR are tactical and reactive in the areas of compliance, compensation and benefits, and employer relations. HR's job is to protect the organization from its people, not to grow the talent within the organization. There is a reason HR is known as a policing function. Because they actually are by function the internal policy police. HR is the complaint and compliance department for a reason. However, when a person launches a complaint, it is usually the first step in the organization making moves to expel that person (now known as a risk) from the organization.

Talent management when done right is a true strategic resource function. For this very reason, in my opinion, it should not be considered traditional HR. It's truly analogous to supply chain management. Figuratively, if you had to look at an X-ray of an organization, what's the one part that would connect to everything and hold it all together? What connects the divisions, to the departments, to the mission, to the vision of the organization? It's the backbone. And in this analogy, that backbone is the people of the organization. Why aren't executives more focused on ensuring that there is an integrated, cohesive effort to manage the very thing that's connects the most important parts of the business and that sustains the organization's existence?

STUCK IN THE MIDDLE

In large companies, with lots of assets and materiel requirements, you've got supply chain management as a critical function and responsibility. Senior Vice President of Supply Chain. What's that job? Simple, to know how, when, and where to get the resources we need to make the products we sell? To be a master of how do we get stuff in and get stuff out? To instinctively know if we have got enough raw materials on the shelf? To be a gatekeeper to make sure we don't buy more than we need? To watch over the supplies to make sure we don't have to worry about pilferage, spoilage, or the supplies being outdated in their use. We do that for widgets. Why not do the same for people? Why aren't we talking about human capital supply chain management? This is the approach to the supply chain approach to talent management as discussed by Peter Cappelli in his book *Talent On Demand: Managing Talent in an Age of Uncertainty.*

I agree with Cappelli's way of thinking and share it with you here. You must admit it makes sense. If talent management is thought about in this way, how could it not be strategic? How could it not be tied to the business strategy of the organization? And more importantly, how could anyone say that this is a traditional HR function that should be left to generalists?

Most corporate management has a balance-sheet mentality. When you talk about monolithic, old school, corporate management from the industrial age, it is very much balance sheet driven. You manage by the numbers, you manage by the line item, but ultimately it's the individuals, it's the people that yield the results that you see in those line items. Why not also think of people as a line item, as a critical aspect of your organization?

It's not like you have to create all new infrastructure. In reality, you've got leaders, executives and managers that are performing that function. You don't need to create a talent management department in your organization. You do however need to inculcate talent management principles within every department of your organization. To do that, you have to have someone who understands talent management, who can translate it, and who can deliver it as actionable items for the organization to follow: *"This is how you do it. This is your blueprint. These are the steps to follow. Here, I will take you by the hand and we will do this together."* I have seen organizations that put the right person in place, who in one year, has worked to create enough culture change in the organization to arrive at measurable results.

The difference between talent management and human resources is simple. Human resources is the tactical, reactive day to day support function that keeps people in line and squelches any threats to the organization by its employees. Talent management on the other had is the strategic, proactive positioning of people to create the current and future bench strength of the organization. From this viewpoint, it becomes easier to not get stuck in the middle between what these two separate functions are in place in the organization to do, and easier to manage expectations.

CHAPTER FIFTEEN

Setting & Following Your Career Path

Be absolutely determined to enjoy what you do.

– Gerry Sikorski

If I had to break down the levels, the first level of leadership is the supervisor and manager level. The middle level is your senior manager, director or senior director. Then there's the executive level... VPs, SVPs, and EVPs, business unit presidents, etc. The Gen Xers that I talk to with that have the most concerns about their own situation and place within an organization are at the supervisor, manager/senior manager, and director/senior director level. They want something known as career pathing. In other words, a detailed plan that they can follow step by step that assures their success in the organization.

Career pathing in and of itself is a great engagement tool, but it's based on the lazy man's guide to having a career. What Gen Xers want —and this also contributes to the bleed that we're seeing in corporate America—is someone to say to them, *"Here's your career path. If you spend three years here with our organization and you do these things, at the end of those three years, you will be well positioned to be a director. At the end of these three more years, you'll be ready for a role as a senior director. At the end of another three years, you'll be in position to become a VP."*

It reminds me of when I was in the Navy, where the amount of time it took to go from E-5 to an E-6, was a defined period of time (three years) before you could sit or take the exam for E-6. The codes and numbers are not important to know, but think about it like going from manager (E-5) to senior manager (E-6). Called "time in grade" in the Navy, it was the waiting period that you had to endure before you could go up for the next level up from your current level. But this wasn't simply a holding pattern. You were expected to gain knowledge, and skills for the next level of promotion. It forced the gaining of practical experience. It forced time on the job. You had to have certain ratings on your annual performance reviews to even be considered for promotion. There was specific field coursework involved, a list of challenging assignments to be completed and signed off on as having being done correctly by your leader, and you had to take an exam with everyone else in the Navy around the world on the same day who was going up for promotion to the next level in your specific job field. Those who received a total score above a determined "cut line" got promoted. Those who didn't make it got feedback in their exam score report. They got to see what areas tripped them up, and an action plan of what to focus on over their wait for the next cycle to come up ... six months later.

No secrets, no drama, no playing favorites, not wondering what you needed to do to get promoted. This was the Navy path to your professional development. The Navy was very structured and in my opinion did an outstanding job in managing the expectations of its employees, and the needs of the organization when it came to talent management. And for those who were happy at any time with their career progression, you know that you could stay where you were. Steady Eddy and Steady Betty were also in the Navy. And they were appreciated for being who they were and how they contributed to their parts of the organization.

This type of promotion and advancement clarity is sorely needed in civilian organizations now more than ever. Gen Xers like it when they have an idea of what they need to do; a checklist that defines what is needed, etc. What you have to be cautious about though, is career pathing could be construed by some that if they just do the things on the list, that they will automatically be promoted to the next level. Organizations, I believe, don't do a good enough job managing that expectation by saying to their employees,

"Yes, doing these things is important. But just because you have completed them there doesn't make promotion automatic. Three things have to happen for you to be promoted: 1) there needs to be an open slot or position. I can't just give you the title; you have to move from one spot to another 2) You have to be seen doing the work of the next higher level before we make you that level, and 3) Other leaders in the organization have to see you working at this level so that there is unilateral support for the suggestion of your promotion or upward movement."

There has to be that level of understanding of the balance of opportunity and preparation for promotion and is the responsibility of the leader to make sure that the process is clear to the employee. If you are a super-proficient manager, but you're not doing any of the tasks or raising your hand for any projects or trying to extend yourself into the next higher level, why would the organization want to promote you to director? You're not showing the organization that you have the desire to be there. This is a flash back to our conversation of demonstrated and expressed ability, aspiration, and engagement. To play that forward, in my opinion, no one should get or expect to get promoted without having all six check marks.

The challenge to that is for the HR community, career pathing is not something on their radar. Most HR generalists in most HR departments do not really have the time to sit down and say, *"Here is a career path from Analyst I, to Analyst II, to Analyst III, and to Analyst IV."* Some leaders will say, *"If HR were more strategic, then it would be on their radar."*

I have to stick up for my HR colleagues and say even if they were to create that, ultimately, it's still up to the business to decide who goes from Analyst I, to Analyst II. Just because you have the "time in grade" doesn't mean there's an opportunity for you to move to that level. Gen Xers assume that just because there's a career path that it guarantees success, and that's not true. You could walk that path and follow everything to the letter and still not have an opportunity, because they don't have a slot for you.

Career success is when opportunity meets preparedness.

You could be the most prepared person in the world for an opportunity, but if the opportunity you want most doesn't come around in your current organization, you've got two choices: wait and hope, or seek and find.

Hope is not a strategy. To be specific, we all know of people who have stayed with organizations for years only to face year after year of disappointment with not being given the career that they wanted or had "hope for" over all those years. A career success strategy is, *"I believe I'm qualified. I'm going to go somewhere else and find the opportunity I know I am prepared for right now."* Gen Xers make those decisions every day, and we have to... or we become our parents.

If I felt like I was prepared to move up and if I was not afforded the opportunity, I left for another opportunity because I knew I was prepared. Every time I left one employer and went to another organization, I walked in a new set of doors at the level I was seeking to get promoted into by my former employer. I have never looked back, I simply tuned the page on my career and moved forward with my head up, shoulders back and eyes open. Sitting and hoping that someone will simply realize your career aspirations and reward you with the career of your dreams is at best unrealistic.

Being prepared is having a well-stocked toolbox. You get your degree and they can't take it away from you. Get professionally certified and they can't take it away from you. Those things that prepare you; they're tools you put in your toolbox. And every toolbox I've ever seen has handles or wheels on it. It goes with you. That's the whole idea. You and your skills are not only valuable to your current organization regardless of how they might try to make you feel or think about yourself, or how lucky they want you to feel you are to work for the company. Your knowledge, your skill, your ability, your expertise and your success to date at company X can lull you into thinking you have to stay there or you will never realize your dream. Your dreams should be company agnostic. Tying your career aspirations to a specific company and having unrealistic expectations of their loyalty is setting yourself up for disappointment.

When a high potential departs an organization, that is a tough retention and engagement hit for organizations because it leaves leaders in the organization saying, *"We spent all this money and time on this person to get them to this place, and now they're going to leave before our plan for them was realized."* In reality, this person is leaving so they can realize their plan for themselves, to pursue their career passion, to own their own succession plan.

It's self-actualization. This is the thing organizations need to realize. If you don't develop that culture of knowing, growing, showing, and flowing talent–giving Gen Xers opportunities, you're going to continually wrestle with untimely loss of them from your organization. You want people to prepare themselves, you want them to go out and get that degree or get that extra education or certification—but if you don't have a system that rewards them with an opportunity to use these new skills—then you have given them a disincentive to develop themselves and a push to leave the company. The only incentive becomes for employees to add new tools to their toolbox as they prepare themselves to leave the company. With the right tools they have everything they need to get unstuck from the middle with you having contributed generously to their inventory.

CHAPTER SIXTEEN
Interviewing for Skill, Hiring for Fit

Look for an occupation that you like, and you will not need to labor for a single day in your life.

–Confucius

Hiring for fit is an important consideration. If you actually do it so that you're not just talking the talk, and you make that as one of the talent management pillars for your workforce, Gen Xers will buy into the importance of fit. They will buy into it with knowledge beforehand of it being part of the process, part of the overall philosophy of people moving and finding their place within the company... or they will leave to find a better personal and career fit with another employer.

This book contains what I feel are quite a few examples of actions you can take to change from being an organization that is continually hitting potholes in the road, to one that finds smooth, open road opportunities for top talent and creates a culture of growth and sustainability. That way, organizationally, you've got the capability to rise above the circumstances. Because you've done the very best job to inspire your main resource, your main driver for your organization, which are your people.

When you talk about talent acquisition, looking at it from a numbers perspective, 70% of organizations have a weak pipeline of talent, in terms of how they plan to bring talented people into the organization.

- The cost per day when operating without a key player can be anywhere from $3,000 to $7,000 a day.
- The cost of a poor hire is between $300k and $500k in terms of an impact.

The challenge for talent acquisition is to not go out and say, *"Here is all the knowledge, skill, and abilities that we need to find."* The organization is not just hiring a resume. It is hiring an entire person, hiring for the best fit with the team while trying to cement a commitment to talent management. It's tough to know an entire person in a series of one-hour interviews. Anybody can be on their best behavior for a scheduled hour by phone or on a couple of days in person. What happens when the whole person shows up day, after day, after day once hired? What happens when the onboarding hits a snag? The questions start immediately: Did we hire the right person? Is the person we hired the right fit for the organization? Did we hire the right combination of knowledge, skill, ability, AND personality in our most recent hire? That's the art about making a right hire. And it is the responsibility of the hiring managers, not the recruiters, to get this crucial task right.

Hire for the best fit, not the best resume.

Recruiters are the ones out there on the front lines of the workforce, trying to bring talent into organizations; there are a lot of qualified people out there from a credential standpoint on the street. Fit is always going to be the challenge. Will this person fit our organization? There are many meanings to that. Does the person look and feel to others like they belong here?

The answers to those questions play a huge role into the talent acquisition success. Unfortunately, recruiting and staffing is seen by the organization as an easy thing, as a lower level skill. On the contrary, it is probably one of the hardest things under the umbrella of talent management to find the right match of talent to the organization and the hiring manager that needs that talent. And organizations sometimes shy away from being very definitive about the type of person that they want, because they don't want to be viewed as being biased in some way. Personally, I think that this is erring too far on the side of political correctness. As a culture and a society, we've carried it way too far.

One of the biggest things that frustrates hiring managers is that recruiters take too long to get the talent that the company needs. In reality, the business doesn't understand what the recruiter is doing. When the hiring manager says,

"I need a human factors engineer. I want them to have 10-12 years' worth of experience. I want them to have worked for one of the big five consulting firms. I want this person to be in the local area, because I'm not paying relocation."

All of these unique factors not only shrink the candidate pool and restricts the options of what the recruiter has to work with, but also increases time to hire.

I am sticking up for recruiters here and acknowledging that this is what they are faced with daily. Once the hiring manager says, *"Do you have everything you need? You're going to get me this person. Great. Thanks. Bye."* The clock starts for the business leader right then and there. In reality, the recruiter takes this information, and has to create the job requirement if it doesn't exist. That might take two or three days to write it, review it, post it, and start to field resume submissions from applicants. It might be three weeks or a month before the recruiter even starts to get candidates in for interviews from when the posting went up based on conversations with the hiring leader. The hiring leader is ticked off. *"It's been two months. Where is this person I need?"* Without constant contact from the recruiter back to the hiring leader, the hiring manager doesn't know the particulars of the situation, or what goes on behind the curtain. They think, *"Next time I will hire an outside agency so that I can get this done in less time!"*

Unfortunately, that's what happens to internal recruiters. They are out there with a flashlight in the middle of the daytime trying to find someone's shadow. They've been given this exacting description of what skills they need to find but they have not had time to get a head start on trying to find that person. And they get very little respect or thanks when they do find the needles in the haystack.

And right now due to the economy, organizations are asking one employee to do the work of two. As such the level of expectation of employers for the same salary is only going up. They want people who can do very special things while carrying a heavy load. That is a challenge. The people who can or would want do these special things exist, but guess what? They're employed. They have a job. They are well paid. They live in another area of the country. Welcome to the new phase of what I believe is recruiting and staffing.

Let's use the example of hunters, fishers, and farmers to describe postures and stances on how to recruit talent. Let's concentrate on hunters and fishers for a moment. We will come back to farmers.

To over simplify what fishers do: they go out there, bait their hook, drop their line in the water and wait. Something comes and it bites on it and they hope it's what they want. They haul it in and, if it is the right fish, everybody wins. That's the old phase of recruiting. Just put a job posting out there, and qualified talent will come and find it. In today's environment, you put your fishing line in the water and you pull up old shoes, tires, everything else. Anything can swim by and get caught on your hook, and when you reel it up, it's not what you want, so you've got to throw it back. That exercise from a metaphorical standpoint can take months, and cost thousands of dollars in wasted time and resources.

Stop being a talent fisher and learn to be a talent hunter.

Go out and hunt, capture and bring back the talent your organization needs. It used to be called recruiting and staffing. However, now it's been more appropriately renamed to talent acquisition. That's what headhunters do. Headhunters make it their business to figure out where the best talent is. They will present opportunities to that talent and say,

"This is what I've got. Do you like it? This is a great next step in your career. It pays $50,000 more a year. It's with a direct competitor of your current company. They will allow you to work from home (or virtually) three days a week. What do you think?"

"Hmm, that sounds pretty good."

Talent gets poached daily just like that. That's what organizations need to realize, but they're not empowering their internal recruiters to do those same things. The recruiters either have to partner themselves with a contingency or retained search firm—these are the real headhunters. These are the active players in the talent management arena.

The thing that's interesting is two aspects of recruiting agency usage can be used to increase the range, and breadth of scope of what your internal recruiting force can do. But agencies need to be used sparingly. From a contingency search standpoint, the recruiter for John Smith Company says, *"We're having a hard time trying to fill this senior vice president role."* They send out a blast to staffing agencies that says, *"The first one of you that brings us the candidate we hire will get 35% of the candidate's annual hiring salary if that person stays for at least six months."* Everybody scatters. The next thing you know—and this is what happens to people that are minding their own business—they get these form emails, phone calls, and LinkedIn messages from headhunters: *"Hey, I've got a great opportunity for this job, this salary, and this company. Send me your resume."* On the other end, this person gets a bunch of resumes and they throw them all over the wall to the hiring managers. Some don't even prep the resume or the hiring manager for what they will receive. They don't even talk to the candidates. They just grab your resume and throw it over the wall to John Smith Corporation. The hiring manager has to sort through this barrage of resumes and decide which candidate they want to interview. The first person that brings on the most qualified candidate that gets hired, six months later, that person gets a payment equal to 35% of the hired candidate's salary. Hooray for the headhunter!

The retained search is actually the more expensive for the company but better for the candidate. The retained search is, *"Okay, 'Jones,' (the headhunter) we want to work with you exclusively. We want you to find us a candidate."*

Jones gets a retainer to go and find this person,

"We need you to find a person within 30 days. We're going to give you $15,000 to put this search at the top of your client stack. Once you find, and we hire that person, within ninety days you'll get 35% of their total hiring compensation."

That's really advantageous to the headhunter, because they're looking for a senior vice president who they will probably pay about $250,000 a year in salary. The headhunter gets 35% of $250,000, plus a $15,000 retainer. Not a bad way to earn a quick $102,500.

The above scenarios are both very costly to the organization. So why do talent acquisition this way? It's a reactionary step caused by a lack of a human capital strategy. It's caused by the lack of true talent management and a strategic work force plan that would have alerted you when you were going to potentially need to replace that person. A very costly mistake is made over and over and here we are only talking about one position.

Organizations should instead invest in learning how to be talent farmers.

For possibly that same cost you just paid for that retained search, you could have had a complete, integrated talent strategy where you would have been able to at least have an inkling of when you would need to replace that person. And you'd probably have it in place where you could build someone to be ready for that role ahead of time for all critical roles and not just one hire.

Organizations will certainly continue to supplement their talent farming efforts with a talent hunter or agency from time to time. But to really to control your costs you have to have total accountability for the process, and have the process in place to support future hiring needs. Organizations have to become talent farmers.

But talent farming is not a quick fix solution. You don't implement that approach thinking, *"It's going to completely solve all of our retention problems or our employee issues over a year."* Now, in a year's time, you may have the foundation laid for something that will help over a five-year period, and certainly longer if you stay the course. Talent farming will instead be a long-term fix. It will be the economic solution that you want. If you were to amortize the cost of implementing a talent farming philosophy you might find that is will take longer, but will be a much lower cost than using staffing agencies exclusively as an extension of your internal recruiters. Which sadly has become more of the routine now leaving the organization's internal recruiters as powerless or being seen as not having the skills they need to bring the talent into the organization as requested. The contingency and retained search model, which when used exclusively, is taking money right out of the pockets of organizations by becoming the hiring managers preferred route to finding, and hiring top talent. The organizations that are about building long-term leadership succession and bench strength philosophy for the organization, buy into a farming approach.

According to metrics attributed research by IBM, in 2008, 2/3 of US employers had no planning efforts for their talent needs. Only 13% of organizations are good at predicting future skills, not just an extension of present ones. What's happened between 2008 and 2011? Crash. Turmoil. Does anyone think clearly long-term when they're in the midst of firefighting? No. So, from 2008 to 2011, these organizations have been fighting fires and trying to just keep the boat afloat.

STUCK IN THE MIDDLE

I think we're coming to a point where things are going to stabilize, because nothing lasts forever—even the downturns, even the bad times. We're going to reach a point of stability. And when that does happen, you will find a lot of organizations that are going to start to think differently. They're not going to ever want to return to talent firefighting, and they're going to turn to thinking, *"We never want to go through that again. We want to at least be able to mitigate our exposure to the whims and vagaries of the markets and economics."* The only way to do that is literally to have as lean and as flexible an organization as possible. That means do more with less. To do more with less, you have to have top talent and processes to enable that talent to do their jobs while pioneering a new paradigm.

You can't do more with less if the people that you've got... those that remain, do not have the capability to pull it off. The best way to find those people is to grow them. You can't hire them; because if you hire them that means that you had to go out and poach them, which costs money and as mentioned earlier is not a long-term solution to a recurring problem. Here are some other facts:

- Forty percent of employees that are on the market right now have been with their current employer less than two years
- Every day, 55,000 baby boomers turn fifty-five-years old
- Sixty percent of jobs in the twenty-first century require skills that are currently possessed by only twenty percent of the workforce
- Seven of the top ten jobs in 2011 didn't even exist in 2004

How does attending college or participating in corporate learning and development programs prepare the workforce for that? That question is a snap back to that 10% of professional development being a learning and development solution. You've got to experience challenges to learn from them. Gen Xers will average 11 to 13 jobs, or positions with as many as eight different employers in their professional career. This news is frightening to most Baby Boomers, while exhilarating to many Gen Xers.

Corporations and organizations over a twenty-year period have had to resign themselves, to hire and replace, hire and replace. If you don't have that talent management that gives Gen Xers comfort enough about their career with your organization, they will go elsewhere, and you will consistently hire and replace, hire and replace. A properly structured talent management strategy such as a "talent farming" strategy can dramatically cut the cost of that impact and can guarantee you perhaps a seven-figure savings over the long run to the company in recruiting and staffing agency costs.

* * *

There are serious questions that companies and organizations must now ask themselves, *"Do we want to continue to muddle along with this talent management thing and have things remain the same?" "Do we want the Board of Directors to continue to kick us to get a plan in place?" "Do we want to put the company into the position where the next time that there's an economic downturn, which there will be, or the competition has a decided advantage and we're losing market share... we can compete." "Do we want to invest in "talent farming" now so that we can have the best talent in house to deal with whatever organizational challenges come next?"*

If not, then they will just stay the same. Admitting that they are not willing to address the hard questions. Admitting that they are not willing to step into the unknown and do things differently. Admitting that this would require people that are self-driven, that have self-confidence, that are willing to get out there and lead.

Don't continue down the path of trying to figure out what accommodates your need to feel comfortable, but is in opposition to the desire to get a result. Because sometimes you have to get uncomfortable to get the result you want. You have to go through a period where it's going to be downright ugly as you shake things up, break things down and build them back up stronger. A sustainable, proactive approach to talent management is the organization's displayed willingness to make lasting cultural change.

Talent management is about sourcing candidates for knowledge, skills, and abilities to accomplish the organization of today's goals. It stresses the importance of hiring based on the right fit for the individual and the organization.

Being stuck in the middle between having employees who are able to do the job, and in a place where they can do the job well is somewhere many organizations often find themselves. Learn to recognize the signs, and to run when you smell the smoke of talent firefighting.

CHAPTER SEVENTEEN

Hope is Not A Strategy

Decide what you want, decide what you are willing to exchange for it. Establish your priorities and go to work.

– H.L. Hunt

There are a lot of books on the topics of business, leadership, management, and self-help on the market written about the power of positive thinking, positive energy and to always have hope.

This is not a book based on hope. This is a book based on taking action. This book is presented to you, the reader, as a tool to put in your career toolbox to keep you as an individual from being stuck in the middle between wishing and hoping for success, and seeking and finding it for yourself.

I believe in having hope and I believe in thinking positively. But I believe more in positive action—in getting things done. You can have dreams and you can get your pad of paper and plan for how they will come true. But unless you start taking action, your plan is worth nothing more that the paper it is written on and ink wasted from your pen. Simply having a plan is not going to result in improvement. Hope is important; it is so powerful of an emotion that it is the motto of the state of Rhode Island where I was born. But hope is not a personal talent management strategy. Hope alone will not help you own your own succession plan.

STUCK IN THE MIDDLE

Some Gen Xers can hope, wish, and dream that they'll grow wings and fly one day; it isn't going to happen. Sometimes the best thing an organization or a leader can do for you is to be honest with you as an employee. To be honest with you and tell you that you are only suited for certain roles, for certain levels of leadership in the organization. This allows you to decide for yourself if you can or want to move beyond your current roles and if you have upward potential with that organization. The company that does this upfront, in an honest, transparent, way... would in my opinion become an employer of choice with Gen Xers. The honesty I speak of would exchange the stale air in the room created from the fetid breath of those who have chosen to wait and hope... for the fresh air of opportunity of those who seek and find their career passion.

Part of making things happen in life, as a company or as an individual, is taking a hard look at things personally and saying, *"These are my flaws. These are my shortcomings. These are self-defeating things I have done to shoot myself in the foot."* Any person or company who says they've never said those things to themselves is not being honest. The unwillingness to do a hard assessment is a disconnect between getting what you want and continuing to lack what you need. Doing it is the magic formula for understanding what it is you really want and then taking the steps to get you that result.

How do you get unstuck?

You, the individual–know what you want. Know what you don't want. For you personally, what makes you happy? What is the difference between what you say you are doing to be successful, and what you're actually doing? If you don't take the time and make the effort to do this and really nail the answers to these questions, you will not get unstuck. Don't wait for anyone to give you what you want or need in your career. Don't look at your career through someone else's eyes. Go out and take the career you desire, own your own succession plan.

You, the company/organization–know what you want. Know what you don't want. When it comes to organizational talent management, learn how to be a farmer and go into it knowing you have to be patient. If you do it right, you will be guaranteed a steady talent crop that will grow and thrive year after year.

Anyone can turn things around if they start with a good, clean understanding. If you don't have that then it's like trying to hire someone to fix things when you don't really buy into the fix itself.

Do the hard thing—look critically at the way things have gone in the past, the way they are presently—and what you want for the future. Admit that there is a gap. Don't accept the status quo. Make things happen for yourself the way you want them to.

When we as Gen Xers don't employ personal talent management by owning our own succession plan; when we as companies and organizations don't build and sustain our bench strength by employing an integrated talent management strategy; we remain stuck in the middle between whom we are and who we want to be. Or perhaps even worse... we fall short of reaching what we have the potential to be.

Getting unstuck begins with asking one of two questions and putting together an action plan (with this book as a guide) to find your own personal answer:

1) If you are stuck in the middle, how will you get yourself unstuck?

STUCK IN THE MIDDLE

2) If you are not stuck in the middle, how will you make sure that you stay unstuck?

ABOUT THE AUTHOR:

Dr. Curtis L. Odom is Principal and Managing Partner of Prescient Talent Strategists.

Curtis brings to Prescient an extensive career history in talent management, performance solutions and organizational change, design and development.

With over 15 years of experience in talent development, performance consulting, training, and instructional design as a practitioner, researcher, author and speaker. He is an expert in strategic planning and tactical application of organizational development, change management, blended learning frameworks and talent management discipline to maximize organizational investments in human capital.

Curtis has an earned doctorate of education from Pepperdine University and has been industry certified as both a Professional in Human Resources (PHR) and a Project Management Professional (PMP) for over 10 years from the Society of Human Resources Management (SHRM) and the Project Management Institute (PMI) respectively.

His additional accomplishments include:

- Certification as both a Human Capital Strategist (HCS) and Strategic Workforce Planner (SWP) from the Human Capital Institute
- Designation as a Professional, Academy of Healthcare Management (PAHM)
- Designation as a Fellow, Academy of Healthcare Management (FAHM)
- Certification from Cornell University as a Certified Diversity Practitioner (CCDP)

- Serving on the Board of Directors of the Northeast Human Resources Association (NEHRA)
- The high distinction of being selected as a member of the Boston Business Journal's Top 40 Under 40 class for 2010

Curtis is a long-standing member of the Internal Society for Performance Improvement (ISPI), the American Society for Training and Development (ASTD), Phi Delta Kappa International Honor Society, the Society for Applied Learning Technology (SALT) and American Mensa. He is also a veteran having served for 10 years in the United States Navy.

Contact Curtis via email at
curtis.odom@prescientstrategists.com

www.ingramcontent.com/pod-product-compliance
Lightning Source LLC
Chambersburg PA
CBHW022038190326
41520CB00008B/630